# The Anti-Jewish Riots in Oslo

# The Anti-Jewish Riots in Oslo

## Eirik Eiglad

You who live safe
In your warm houses,
You who return in the evening to find
Hot food and friendly faces:

Consider if this is a man,
Who works in the mud,
Who does not know peace,
Who fights for a scrap of bread,
Who dies because of a yes or a no.

Consider if this is a woman,
Without hair and without name,
With no more strength to remember,
Her eyes empty and her womb cold,
Like a frog in winter.

Consider that this has been:
I commend these words to you.
Engrave them on your hearts
When you are in your house, when you walk on your way,
When you go to bed, when you rise,
Repeat them to your children.

Or may your house crumble,
Disease render you powerless,
Your offspring avert their faces from you.

*– Primo Levi, 1946*

*The Anti-Jewish Riots in Oslo*
2010 © by Eirik Eiglad

ISBN 978-82-93064-00-8
Published by Communalism Press

Check our website: http://www.communalism.net

*Communalism*
Grenmarsvegen 12,
N–3912 Porsgrunn,
Norway

In addition to books and pamphlets, we publish *Communalism:
A Social Ecology Journal* (ISSN 1891–540x; Three issues a year,
subscriptions are available). Contact us for distribution.

Design and layout by Eirik Eiglad. Cover photo, "Kill the Zionists,"
by Peter A. Kristoffersen. Primo Levi's poem, "Shemà," was
translated by Ruth Feldman and Brian Swann.

# Contents

# Introduction

One year ago, Oslo experienced an alarming outburst of anti-Jewish anger. As a humanist and an antifascist, I was profoundly shaken by the events; I never thought I would live to see anti-Jewish riots in the Norwegian capital.

Before I ask you to re-experience those days with me, I need to clarify some issues. First of all, I am neither a Zionist nor a nationalist of any sort. Secondly, I do not, in any sense, accept the simplistic and xenophobic analyses and solutions presented by right-wing populists and reactionaries. Although I am highly critical of the Norwegian Left, it is from a *leftist* perspective. I am a social ecologist, believing in direct democracy, the Enlightenment, and a libertarian form of socialism.

I was genuinely shocked to witness the events unfold. But no one should believe that I was so traumatized as to reach rash political conclusions: on the contrary, the events impelled me, not to change my political views, but to speak out. I have been struggling with these issues since I became radicalized in the early 1990s. If anything, I apologize for dealing with the frustratingly complex issues in the Middle East only in passing; there are undeniably more nuances to this conflict than can be possibly conveyed within such a short narrative.

On a January weekend in Oslo, the war against Hamas was used as a pretext to unleash hate attacks of the vilest sort. Yes, people were definitely angry at the Israeli bombing and the ensuing ground invasion. Yet much of the hatred expressed in Oslo went far deeper than objections to the invasion of Gaza; it points to tendencies far beyond the question of Israel's policies.

Some readers may suggest that I have highlighted only the worst. I have tried not to. I do, however, insist that some contemporary political actions and expressions follow distinct – although sometimes subtle – historical, cultural, and ideological patterns. Without putting them in *context*, we cannot understand these actions and expressions. Too often, in general, we do not reflect on where our ideas come from and what conclusions they lead to. This is not only ideologically confusing, but politically dangerous.

My account is not intended as an exhaustive report on contemporary anti-Semitism in Norway: it is only about the riots that took place on a particular weekend. I wrote this account one month after the events, and in the year that has passed, many related incidents have occurred that also warrant serious attention and reflection. I would argue, however, that these riots marked a real watershed in Norway's troubled relationship with Israel and Palestine. That intense weekend, some very important lines were crossed.

Some readers may find it problematic or even arrogant that I do not, in any substantial way, address or present a social analysis of what may seem to be the main actors of the riots, namely immigrant youths. For a larger work examining anti-Semitic trends and developments in Norwegian society, this would be both welcome and necessary, but it falls outside the purview of this essay. Here I have dealt with these actors only to the extent that they did *act* in these events, and have challenged their opinions only when they expressly voiced them. Hate crimes, I firmly believe, should not be "explained away" – they should be exposed and confronted, regardless of who commits them.

My account is neither meant to be academic nor even overly theoretical. I have written about the events as I experienced them and reflected upon them. For readability, I have kept my references to an absolute minimum: For the most part, I have used footnotes only in reference to videos that are available on the Internet, so that readers may see with their own eyes what Oslo was like for a few freezing days in January 2009. (A collection of hyperlinks is available in an online version at www.communalism.net.)

However, to provide a fuller picture of the challenges we face, I have supplemented my narrative with two appendixes. In Appendix 1, I list some general principles that leftists – particularly left-libertarians – should have in mind when dealing with questions of Israel and anti-Semitism. Appendix 2 contains a list of easily accessible books and documentaries that may give the concerned reader a better overview of political realities and ideological patterns. Plenty of information is available for those who care to look.

I would like to use this opportunity to thank my co-editors Sveinung Legard, Camilla Svendsen Skriung and Andy Price. I am also grateful for helpful comments by Kjetil B. Simonsen, Peter A. Kristoffersen, Thodoris Velissaris, Jostein Køhn, Kim Andre Næss, Peter Zegers, Jonathan Korsár, Giorgio Giusti, Yngvild Hasvik, Maria Rosvoll, Nicolas Schwaller, Michael Speitel, Peter Munsterman, and last, but not least, Janet Biehl. All errors and opinions are of course my own.

More than simply engendering controversy, I hope this book will encourage self-reflection and serve as a sobering warning. I was there, present during the whole weekend, and this is how I experienced it.


Eirik Eiglad
January 8, 2010

# *I Have Seen the Future*

I was visiting Oslo for a few days, hoping to get some writing done in a place where I could concentrate, without distractions. After a while, needing a break, I called my friend Kjetil. We had both heard about several events that were planned for downtown that evening, and were curious about them, so we agreed to meet there. The war in Gaza was going on, and it had received massive media attention. This evening, three demonstrations were to take place. One was in support of Israel's right to self-defense and its declared war on Hamas; the second was to be a counterdemonstration, organized by supporters of the Palestinian cause. Both were to take place in the square that lies before the Norwegian Parliament building (Stortinget). Later that evening a third event, a torch-lit protest with more general calls for peace, was to take place at another central square, Youngstorget.

For many years I had been reluctant to participate in demonstrations around the Middle East, as their nationalist overtones tend to obscure or even contradict the more fundamental message of social liberation. So I usually stay away.

That Thursday, however, curiosity lured me out of the apartment.

As I stepped into the biting cold January afternoon, I wished I had put on more layers of clothing. Shivering as I approached the Parliament, I passed Anne Sender, president of the Norwegian Jewish Community. I recognized her from her many televised interviews; since the war on Hamas had started, she had had to explain over and over again that Jews in Norway actually hold a variety of political views. Now she was waiting for someone on a street corner, with an anxious look on her face.

Continuing, I passed several information stalls featuring numerous posters with large close-ups of bloodied and dead children, captioned "Stop the Massacres in Gaza" and "End Israel's Terror." Market vendors had told reporters that the public demand for the keffiyeh – the traditional Arab headdress – was explosive, so eager were Norwegians to display their support for the Palestinian cause. The word *explosive* is no understatement: hurrying through the streets of Oslo, I saw people from all walks of life wearing this symbol. It suddenly struck me how long it was since I had seen anyone publicly wearing a Star of David.

I arrived at the square at 16.30, about half an hour before the two demonstrations were both supposed to start. For days the media had been reporting that some kind of trouble was brewing, so the riot police were prepared: they had set up a riot fence to separate the two demonstrations and were heavily guarding it. The side near busy Karl Johan Street was already simmering, as pro-Palestinian protesters were gathering, enough to form a crowd, mixing with waves of ordinary citizens passing through.

Pulled by curiosity, I eased toward the pro-Palestinian crowd. A woman yelled at me and other passersby, urging us to remember the Second World War and Norwegian resistance to the Nazi occupation. "Israel now behaves just like the Nazis," she cried. "We are fighting the occupation force, just like you [Norwegians] did."

Skeptical, I hurried past her and burrowed further into the now-dense crowd. Many people were carrying large photographs of dead children. Arrayed along the riot fence, facing the pro-Israeli demonstrators, aggressive protesters were denouncing "child murderers." Other parts of the crowd were stridently chanting "Israel: terrorist!" Feeling uneasy, I left the square and crossed to try to find a quieter place down the street.

There I encountered a few Maoists handing out leaflets, calling on us to "crush Israel" and denying its legitimacy as a state; the point was illustrated by the notoriously anti-Semitic Brazilian artist Carlos Latuff.[1] Without mentioning Hamas by name, the leaflet asked us to "stop condemning

1. This leaflet is available in Norwegian here: http://www.tjen-folket.no/uploaded_images/420-full.pdf. Despite his virulent anti-Semitic imagery, Latuff is widely published by alternative, progressive, leftist-oriented publications around the world.

the armed Palestinian resistance." Judging from the placards and the slogans I'd just seen at the pro-Palestinian demonstration, this leaflet captured its message: Hamas was the resistance movement, and its actions were just.

I'd done some reading on the Middle East and knew that the name *Hamas* is an acronym for Islamic Resistance Movement (*Harakat al-Muqāwamat al-Islāmiyyah*); the jihadist organization has sworn merciless war against Israel and Jews. But the Maoists gave me my first revelation of the weekend: that the pro-Palestinian demonstration was not only challenging the war in Gaza and current Israeli policies; it was intransigently *anti*-Israel, and – perhaps despite the intentions of many of its participants – distinctly *pro*-Hamas.

Uncomfortable, I moved away, as I did not want anyone to think that I supported these views. I did not want even my silent presence to be taken as tacit support for Hamas.

On the other side of the square were assembled the supporters of Israel. But the riot fence closed off that side of the square. I asked a policewoman whether there was any way of getting inside. "Yes, over there," she said, pointing toward a far corner. I couldn't see it but headed that way. By now I'd seen no signs of Kjetil, so I tried calling his cell – no answer.

Finally the opening in the riot fence came into view – but once I reached it, I hesitated to enter. After all, the main speaker was to be Siv Jensen, the leader of the right-wing Progress Party (Fremskrittspartiet). Jensen is at the opposite end of the political spectrum from me, with my libertarian socialist convictions. But my curiosity impelled me to make my way through the two-foot-wide entrance, past a group of police officers and two young guards with reflective yellow vests. Anxiously I took in the crowd, who were waving blue and white Israeli flags. Most of them seemed to have come from Christian congregations, bused in from the Norwegian Bible Belt; they had their own peculiar – in my view, highly problematic – religious motivations for defending Israel. Not all Christians share those sentiments, of course – a few days earlier, the former bishop of Oslo, Gunnar Stålsett, had denounced support for Israel as "un-Christian."

The menacing shouts and slogans from the pro-Palestinian demonstration could be heard here and were impossible to ignore. Probably only those pro-Israelis with particularly strong political convictions had dared to show up that day. I pushed through the crowd, but it felt awkward, and I soon headed back toward the fence.

On my way out, seeing how the angry crowds were hammering at the fence, I wondered whether the pro-Israelis inside were fenced in, or whether the anti-Israelis outside were fenced off. At any rate, having one's security depending on the muscles of a strong police cordon was rather unpleasant.

Because it was so cold, I hurried around the neighborhood to try to generate some heat. Snow had not yet fallen on the capital, but icy winds whipped through the streets. In

Karl Johan Street, the police arrived in large riot vans and parked at the fence, making a more solid wall to protect the pro-Israelis. And now they needed protection: bottles and small rocks were being thrown at them. The pro-Palestinian crowd was steadily growing, but as it was located in a busy street, I could not tell how big it really was. Neither could I tell whether most people on the pro-Palestinian side were there to show support for Hamas or were mere passersby – or something in between.

One thing was clear: those who did not display unconditional support for the Hamas "resistance" simply disappeared in the crowd, whose blatant denunciations of Israel were both audible and visible. Many from this side were trying to get through the fence that the police defended; amid the turbulence the slogan "Israel: terrorist!" was chanted steadily, rhythmically.

Finally I reached Kjetil by phone – he said he would meet me downtown as soon as he picked up his one-year-old son. I went over to quiet end of the square, toward Parliament Street (Stortingsgaten), and from that distance watched the two demonstrations unfold. The influx of pro-Israeli sympathizers squeezing through the guarded opening to their side was steady; pro-Palestinian protesters were trying to get through too, but the police repeatedly turned them away. Standing at the opening, they openly harassed people inside. As I watched, a few seemed about to try, then decided not to enter, evidently fearing trouble.

Some ten meters from me a group of pro-Palestinian protesters tried to mount the riot fence, crying "fascists" and "Zionists." The police beat them back with clubs. Thereafter I noticed a sinister change: many of these protesters turned their attention to solitary individuals standing outside the cordon. As they couldn't attack the pro-Israeli demonstration directly, they looked for individuals who seemed to harbor those sympathies.

Some of these people cruised around me. I was standing next to an old man with a gray coat and sad eyes – he was visibly distressed.

Then things happened fast.

A man of about forty with wavy brown hair passed me heading toward the entrance, carrying a small Israeli flag. An angry group that had gathered a few meters from me physically stopped him. "Zionist!" they cried. "You support the massacres!" They pushed him and were very aggressive.

As the group was about to encircle him, I couldn't watch their bullying anymore. Before I could reflect too much, I took a few steps forward and planted myself next to the man, on his right side.

At first the group was small, but the commotion they made soon attracted more, until the core group had about 15 or 20 people, with more scattered around them. Most seemed to be first- or second-generation immigrants. Several were girls of high school age wearing *hijabs*, but most were boys aged 15 to 30 wearing the *keffiyeh*, some to fully mask their faces.

As I was standing there, they first paid little attention to me, but kept screaming at the brown-haired man, pulling his blue jacket and shoving him around. His only response to their harassment was "I am not looking for trouble."

Soon he was able to climb over the riot fence. I saw him straighten his jacket and enter the pro-Israeli demonstration.

As soon as he was gone, the crowd turned to me and started bullying me. My back was pressed up against the riot fence, but I didn't want to climb over it. I had tried the other demonstration earlier and I did not want to join it. The way this conflict was framed, I honestly did not want to take sides. Neither did I want to back down or to excuse myself. From the corner of my eye, I noticed with relief that the gray-eyed old man had vanished.

The young people hurled accusations at me: "You support the Zionist murders!" They called me a "racist," "fascist," and "child murderer," and they blamed me for being a "Zionist" and even a "Jew!"

"How can you support the massacres?" they all asked in various ways. "How can you defend the killing of innocent children?" I had not voiced any opinion at all, and in my black hoodie and worn Icelandic woolen sweater, I must have looked like a stereotypical Norwegian leftist Palestine-supporter. All I had done was defiantly place myself next to a random victim. Everyone in the group cursed me and bombarded me with epithets like "Zionist" and "child murderer."

I surveyed them, looking them in the eyes, hoping to defuse the situation. But they were in a lynching mood and kept pushing and insulting me.

"Come with me," said one of the older ones, a well-built man of about 35. "Come into the alley over there" – he pointed with his thumb – "and I'll show you what to do with Zionists." His gesture conveyed clearly what he meant.

"This is cowardice," I replied calmly.

I was appalled by their behavior and too proud to back down. The older chap once more challenged me to cross the street with him: "I'll show you how who is the coward," he said. "Coward," I said again, this time to him, doing my best to stay calm. All the while they maligned me intensely. As I did nothing to return their provocations, they gradually dispersed, and even several of the militants left.

Then the man who had threatened to beat me up in a dark alley spat a large gob in my face, and pulled away. A man of about 25, almost bald with deep sunken cheeks, came in from the left and pushed me and spat at me in the face. One of the younger ones jumped in from the right and gave me a solid kick in the balls. I gasped but fortunately managed to stand erect. Still I did not respond to their provocations. By now, more and more were finding me uninteresting as a target, and soon only a few were left. I received one last gob of spit, and they dashed off to find more action. Most went down to Rosencrantz Street, at one side of the square, where the situation was growing very tense.

When they were all gone, I wiped the spit from my face with my sleeve and turned to lean on the fence again. From this position I could watch the demonstrations.

I felt intensely estranged. Had extremist hatred really gone this far? Here, in Norway? As a longtime antinationalist and a committed antistatist, my choice to take no sides in this conflict had been a conscious one: after all, how could I defend either state? The ultimate solution, I believed (and still do), lay elsewhere. Now, not only had I witnessed attacks on a random victim, but I had been personally attacked, by people who believed that I was a Zionist or – God forbid! – a Jew. Yet the kids who had attacked me knew nothing of my ideas or my background.

As the reality dawned upon me, I grew angry and disgusted. I felt like going home but decided to stay a little longer. After all, I had a ringside view of the madness, and I had yet to meet Kjetil.

The voices of the speakers from one side of the fence were drowned by the tumultuous cacophony on the other, always to the steady beat of the chant "Israel: terrorist!"

Cries "*Allahu Akbar*" now could be heard, as well as the denunciations of "terroristic Israel." Two people strode past me, carrying the yellow flag of Hezbollah, eager to join the demonstrating crowd. *That's it!* I said to myself. This is *not* acceptable – *This is insane.*

I kept waiting near the fence, and the rain of bottles and small rocks intensified.

Some fifteen minutes later one of the youths returned. He was not masked: a handsome young man, perhaps 18 years old, he was in no way threatening now.

"Are you a Jew?" he asked me in fluent Norwegian.

I just gave him a skeptical look, raising an eyebrow.

He asked me a second time.

I answered calmly, almost slowly, "*Why* do you ask?"

"Well, I am just wondering whether you are from this country, or whether you are Jewish."

Because I don't have the fair complexion of the stereotypical Norwegian, I've often been mistaken for someone of southern European origin, perhaps from France or Italy. Still, this question was different.

"No, I'm not," I answered, but then felt stupid. "Not that it matters," I immediately added. The mob he had been standing with earlier had accused me of being a Jew, a Zionist, and a racist, for placing myself quietly next to one of their random victims.

"So why do you defend this?" he asked, pointing toward the pro-Israeli demonstration. "Why do you defend these people?"

I was in no mood for a political discussion, but he seemed sincere, and his eyes met mine – always a good sign.

"Are you *really* interested?" I asked.

"Yes, I am," he said. "I don't defend what happened to you earlier."

"It's still happening." I nodded toward the barrage of bottles and stones.

"I don't defend that either," he admitted, "but it's important to protest." Then he challenged me: "How can you defend how they are killing children?"

At that moment another young man from the mob returned, obviously a friend or acquaintance. He had covered his whole face with the keffiyeh, so that only his eyes were visible. He came up to me with aggressive gestures and asked obstinately: "Yes, what do you think? Why are you defending these Jews?"

*A ninja!* I thought. *They must be kidding.* I was still unenthusiastic about the prospects of a political discussion – these adrenaline-fired kids were clearly just looking for trouble. I turned to him. "Just back off!" I said firmly. "I'm not interested in talking to *you*. Get lost!"

"You have to respect us," he said.

"This isn't about lack of respect," I said. "You don't understand a thing. Now back off!"

The other kid told him, more gently, to leave. Our young ninja-wannabe then left.

"If you are genuinely interested in my opinions," I said, "I don't wish to defend either side. I prefer a different kind of politics.

"*But,*" I added, "I know for certain that it won't be possible to reach any kind of peace in the Middle East until the Palestinians get rid of Hamas, which does not seek a solution to the conflict. They've even said they don't want to honor any agreement short of regaining 'Palestine' from the river Jordan to the sea."

The police inside the fence were putting on their gas masks. So were the many journalists on the scene.

"As a matter of fact," I continued, "Hamas wants to get rid of all Jews from the Middle East and create an Islamic state based on Sharia. That won't benefit Palestinians, or Jews, or anyone else for that matter." Hamas was, after all, a jihadist and Islamist political party. Thinking of Ibn Warraq's words, "Muslims are the first victims of Islam," I tried turning the tables: "Hamas isn't a liberation movement. How can you be here, supporting *them*?"

"I don't support everything Hamas does," was his brief response.

By now, I was all fired up. "I really find it immensely tragic," I said, "that so many Palestinian Arabs support this authoritarian and anti-Semitic organization, which was founded on a religious form of fascism. It's not possible to conclude any peace as long as one part seeks to eradicate Israel and wipe out all Jews."

"Hamas doesn't want to kill all Jews," he replied.

"Oh yes, they do!" I said. "And they're quite explicit about it in their Charter. They want to remove the Jews, to kill them. There will come a day, they say – and they are actually quoting the Quran – when even stones and trees will rebel against the Jews. The stones and trees will apparently say 'Muslims, behind me a Jew is hiding. Kill him.'"

"Yeah, well, that's actually true," he admitted, visibly surprised that I knew the Charter. "I don't support Hamas, but it's important to show our resistance to Israeli killing of civilians."

"I can agree to that," I said empathically, "but then you *must* also distance yourself from Hamas. They're contributing to the civilian toll. They're using civilians as human shields. They fire their weapons from crowded areas and then hide among civilians. They've even hidden weapon caches in mosques and in schools – this is not exactly a secret. I can agree with you that the loss of civilian lives is tragic, but if you want an end to it, then you have to distance yourself from Hamas and their brutal tactics. They even send civilians up onto rooftops that the Israeli intelligence has just informed them will be bombed."

"Yes, I know," was his only reply.

Evidently we wouldn't get much further in this conversation, as my new friend now seemed distracted by a commotion in the street. The situation intensified, with occasional clashes with police over the fence. He was clearly drawn toward it, but he said, as if in conclusion, "The most important thing is to stop this war."

"Palestinians must remove Hamas," I said. "Until they do, no peace is possible."

I offered him my hand, and he shook it. Then he was gone.

Eggs, bottles, and rocks continued to rain on the pro-Israeli demonstration, hitting many people, hurting some. The cry "*Allahu Akbar*" was becoming more frequent. I later saw reports that "Hamas, Hamas" was chanted.

Next to me by the fence, a woman commented laconically, "Sometimes enthusiasm works against its purpose." Oslo had become surreal.

Farther up the street a blond woman with glasses and a red jacket was desperately clutching the fence, screaming indignantly to the people inside. "You are fascists and racists!" was all I managed to grasp of her message – and I really tried to catch her words.

One of her friends furiously denounced the supporters of "a fascist state that murders children." Numerous times he yelled "*Sieg heil!*" while raising his right arm in a Nazi salute.

Nobody intervened.

I abandoned my place at the fence and found a bookstore to buy a pencil and a small notebook – I wanted to make some notes. The whole scene had shaken me profoundly.

Then Kjetil arrived, with his son; we met in Karl Johan Street, some 150 meters from the square. We were making a cautious plan to take a closer look, but suddenly we heard the police firing canisters of tear gas into the crowd. This was no place for a child, so we went in the other direction, away from the gas and the whole conflict.

As we pushed the stroller, I briefed Kjetil on what I'd seen. He'd done some research on the relationship between anti-Semitism and the Norwegian peasant movement during the interwar period, and so he understood my concern. "Here in Oslo we've seen this coming for years," he told me. "The Left doesn't care – they allow all kinds of banners and slogans to appear in their demos. We've seen this tendency for many years now."

I'd never lived in Oslo for any long period, but Kjetil had. Years back he used to participate in pro-Palestinian rallies, to show his support for their plight and their hardships.

"But the right-wing parties," I added with frustration, "seek only to profit from popular xenophobia and the quite legitimate fear of *Islamism* by trying to blame this extremism on all Muslims, stigmatizing them and criminalizing them. They just aggravate the tensions."

There are many sound reasons to be worried about the extremist and hateful message of *political Islam* – and of jihadism – but they are used to blame Islam as such. Islamophobia has been much discussed recent years, as the right-wingers have done their utmost to collectively blame immigrants, particularly Muslims. That serves only to undermine our struggle for an open, inclusive society.

We talked about Geert Wilders's film, *Fitna*, which was a perfect example. Wilders even compares the Quran to Hitler's *Mein Kampf*. The Quran, of course, is no more regressive than other "holy" books; the problem is that many Islamists insist on a strict interpretation of the book, with unsavory political consequences. Said Kjetil, "They want to turn their religious dogmas into a political ideology, and that is damn dangerous."

"Of course, every religious concept or dogma can be used for reactionary ends," I said. "Opus Dei is very different from Liberation Theology in Latin America, but both are interpretations of the Catholic faith."

The Muslim Brotherhood was formed in Egypt by Hassan al-Banna in 1928 and was introduced into Palestine in 1936. Decades later Abdullah Yusuf Azzam – an influential Palestinian Sunni theologian – and others from the Muslim Brotherhood insisted on an extroverted interpretation of the concept of Jihad that politicized the Islamic faith. Their aim was to rally believers in a political struggle to defend Muslims, to restore Muslim lands from foreign domination, and to uphold the Muslim faith strictly according to the Quran. Politically, the consequences were out-and-out reactionary: Azzam was famous for his slogan, "Jihad and the rifle alone: no negotiations, no conferences, and no dialogues," and for organizing the Arab-Afghan *jihadis*. He influenced the founding of Hamas, itself a wing of the Muslim Brotherhood, and specifically wrote, "The Palestinian problem will be solved only through Jihad."

Many Muslims oppose political Islam and seek instead a reformation of the faith and a secularization of our societies. Some who call themselves "cultural Muslims" are even atheists. I have often felt that the Left has not done enough to support these trends, and especially the groups and individuals that bravely advance humanism and atheism, not to speak of the rights of women, homosexuals, workers, dissenters, and marginalized groups, in Muslim countries.

"It's strange," I said to Kjetil. "Both the Left and the Right portray Muslims as a compact mass of believers." With Orwellian logic, this gray mass is portrayed either as an enemy or as a victim: either Muslims are to be feared or they deserve our unconditional support. "Four legs good. Two legs bad." Or vice versa.

"It shouldn't be impossible to be nuanced yet principled at the same time," Kjetil mused. What could be a solid argument for defending the Enlightenment and an open, inclusive society is instead exploited by Wilders and his ilk to kindle the flames of xenophobia. We both feared that the Right would try to benefit from the events of that night. "I sure hope the Left will be able to counter this upsurge of anti-Semitic hatred," I said. "Maybe this will be the wake-up call." But I wasn't convinced of my own words.

As we passed through the glaring light from neon signs and bright shop windows, I explained how difficult it had been for me over there, caught between hell and a hot place, between Hamas supporters and the Christian Right. After recapping my argument with the protester, I had run out of things to say. Words could not properly convey my intense alienation and powerlessness.

"It is so sickening," was all I said.

"Yes," Kjetil answered solemnly. "It is sickening."

We went over to Main Street and sat down to eat a falafel at Habibi's, while we awaited the next event, the torch-lit "peace march." During this interlude, I managed to buy myself a pair of long underwear. A poor compensation for the evening perhaps, but at least I was no longer cold.

Kjetil went home with his son, and although I was no longer in the mood for the peace rally, curiosity drove me, reluctantly, to Youngstorget to check it out. Here a veritable sea of people were protesting "the war," probably more than ten thousand. I did not get a good picture of the situation, just heard fragments of the speeches, which placed the blame for the war squarely on Israeli shoulders.

Then a speaker asked us to applaud two doctors, Mads Gilbert and Erik Fosse, who were then at the Shifa hospital in Gaza City. Acting as "embedded reporters," these doctors had condemned Israel and minimized the shortcomings of Hamas at every possible juncture. The two have a long history of "anti-imperialist" activism. Indeed, as Gilbert once remarked, "there is *little* in medicine that isn't politics." Gilbert made headlines in 2001 when he defended the attack on World Trade Center, saying that the oppressed had a moral right to strike back.

As for Fosse, in the mid-1980s he had actively called on leftists to support Khomeini's regime. In the pages of *Klassekampen* he praised Iran for detaching itself from Western and Soviet imperialism "not only economically, but culturally and socially." He dismissed the Iranian Sharia laws and the degradation of women as mere "flawed and distorted fractions of the culture," and he ridiculed progressive educational campaigns and women's liberation efforts in Afghanistan, as a "political mission" to colonize the culture. "All mystical, negative, and perhaps brutal aspects of Islamic culture are emphasized and portrayed as reactionary," he complained. Objecting to such abuses is apparently, to this staunch anti-imperialist, "cultural oppression." "The struggle for an Islamic culture," he said, "is central in the struggle for liberation."[2]

The crowd at Youngstorget accorded Gilbert and Fosse thunderous applause. I left. I had seen enough.

Later I learned that this rally did more than call for "peace." According to witnesses who know Arabic, participants voiced blatant anti-Semitic slogans: "Kill the Jews!" "Slaughter the Jews!" and "Go get them!" One leaflet,

---

2.   These quotes are from *Klassekampen* 19 October 1985 and 2 December 1985.

distributed there, recommended that people "empty their trash outside the synagogue" and "place pig heads on the Jewish cemetery." The high-profile Jews Anne Sender and Rabbi Joav Melchior were ousted from this "peaceful" demonstration. Melchior was told, "Damn Jew, get lost!"

That night I stayed out late with friends. When I got home, I searched the Internet for its reportage. As I had feared, there had indeed been further attacks. I had seen restless youth groups zigzagging among the bystanders, apparently looking for Jews upon whom to vent their hatred of Israel. The online newspapers reported several incidents in which mobs had attacked individuals at random. Several people had been shoved, and some had been hit. Sixty-two-year-old Jon Gunnar Aksnes tried to help someone who had been attacked, but was beaten down, his arm fractured in four places.

The following day *Dagbladet* would present a video online that shows youths harassing and attacking a 73-year-old man, Sverre Martin Haug, who had been carrying an Israeli flag. They had pushed him and then kicked him to the ground while yelling "Bloody Jew! Get him!"[3] Two young men, reportedly Muslims, escorted Haug to safety at a Burger King. Interestingly, the video catches the youths deciding against hurting him further not only because "he's old," but mainly because "he's Norwegian," and "not a Jew."

---

3. See http://www.dagbladet.no/2009/01/09/nyheter/opptoyer/krigen_i_
gaza/4312704/.

Presumably, Haug would have made a legitimate target if he had happened to be Jewish.

I had long suspected that anti-Zionism had become the dominant form of anti-Semitism today. Anti-Semitism, I knew, did not die with Himmler, the Nazi state, and its death camps; nor has the subsequent emergence of the state of Israel diminished it. But its new disguises had been less familiar to me, as they may still be to others. Critics of Israel often stress that they distinguish between "anti-Zionism," "anti-Semitism," and hatred of Jews. And certainly traditional Christian anti-Judaism is not the same as racially motivated anti-Semitism. But the similarities are many, and in practical terms mere semantics cannot distinguish them.

In my experience, even moderate anti-Zionists allow for violent expressions of hatred against "Jews" by singling out Zionism – Jewish nationalism – as a particularly crude form of nationalism.

In today's anti-Zionism the "Jewish entity" – Israel, and Zionism – supplants the Jew as an object of extreme hatred. But even "politically correct" anti-Zionism shares many of the characteristics of older forms of anti-Semitism. A glance at Latuff's caricatures, or at the Maoists' anti-Zionist leaflet that night, should be enough to convince anyone that the demarcation lines are blurred.

Not only does anti-Zionism demonize Israel demonized the way earlier anti-Semitism demonized Jews; it denies Israel the right to self-determination and even existence. Just as older anti-Semitism denies Jews the right to exist, today anti-Zionism uniquely denies them the right to form a political entity. And perhaps most important, anti-Zionism now personifies Israel as the international menace, one that even threatens world peace. No other national entity is so targeted by myths and prejudice. During the war against Hezbollah in 2006, the best-selling Norwegian author Jostein Gaarder declared that Israel "has lost its right to exist." In his notorious article, Gaarder amply demonstrated the blurred transition between old anti-Judaist myths and modern anti-Zionist discourse.

I fail to see how anti-Zionism is anything but a regressive expression of the old hatred of Jews. One might have expected an antistatist and antinationalist like me to welcome this form of antinationalism. But anti-Zionism is a *most peculiar* antinationalism. Indeed, it is usually merely another form of nationalism, albeit one that denies Israeli political identity. Hence the sight of crowds burning Israeli flags, particularly while carrying other national flags, is painful. The more I reflect upon it, the more I find it sickening.

The Thursday-night attacks, whether they were directed at alleged Zionists, Israelis, or Jews, were all repulsive. Having combed through all the news reports on that night, I concluded that many lesser confrontations were not properly documented. Not only were random individual "Zionists" attacked; a journalist was hit across the head with a metal bar, and when other journalists rushed to help him, a small Molotov cocktail was thrown at them.[4] In another video of the night's events, a group of youths smashes a police car while yelling "*Allahu Akbar!*" and "child murderers."[5]

Several groups left the parliament square and went over to the Israeli embassy, apparently responding to calls to burn it. When they found police heavily guarding the embassy, they chose instead to smash the windows of a nearby beauty salon – all the while shouting *homophobic* remarks. The salon, as it happens, belongs to a celebrity gay man, Jan Thomas, whose front windows had been smashed in earlier that week during an anti-Israeli demonstration. Another neighbor of the embassy, a public relations agency, had put up posters in its windows saying, "Please *do not* smash more windows! (Go Palestine)." To my knowledge, Jan Thomas had never publicly voiced support for Israeli actions, nor expressed any other controversial political opinion.

The attack on his salon was even more frightening because Mahmoud Zahar, one of Hamas's leaders, has said that in Hamas's Palestine "homosexuals and lesbians" will be defined as "a minority of moral and mental deviants," without any rights.

Is it for this that anti-Israelis fight here in Oslo? Are they perhaps ready to side with the Iranian president, Mahmoud Ahmadinejad, who made the seemingly naïve

---

4.  See http://atvs.vg.no/player/?id=20636.
5.  See http://www.dagbladet.no/tv/index.html?clipid=30199.

but unnervingly brutal statement that "in Iran, there are no homosexuals"?

Few seemed to grasp the significance of these homophobic attacks on Jan Thomas's studio, least of all the "anti-imperialist" Left. "We congratulate!" was the simple and shameless response on the Maoist website Frontlinjer.

Finally in bed, I lay awake for hours. As a humanist, I found the riots too frightening and too embarrassing. Frustrations with the war in Gaza and support for Palestine had crossed over into legitimizing anti-Semitism and hate crimes.

How could I make sense of this development? A few days earlier one anarcho-communist had told me that he thought such protests were fruitful because they "radicalized" youth. Well, some political protests certainly have that effect. But these riots had clear reactionary and anti-Jewish intentions. Whatever "radicalization" they might produce was none that I wanted to see. I am unable to find anything at all progressive about the riots.

They were distinctly anti-Jewish. It is that simple. No euphemism can conceal it, and no excuse can justify it.

As I looked out into the darkness of the city, the voice of Leonard Cohen whispered out of my laptop speaker, singing, "I have seen the future, brother: it is murder."

# *Blitzkrieg Bop*

"It was all planned in advance," Kim told me.

Hearing that I was in the city, he had called to catch up with me. Kim is a friend from my hometown: we share an interest in music, beer, and politics. He too had been downtown during the riots.

When I told him I'd been attacked, he said, "It sure did get out of hand." Evidently many had decided they wanted to see some action.

"Many wanted the counter-demonstration to turn into a riot," he said. And then he told me how people had mobilized for the riots in advance of Thursday.

"I noticed it on several Facebook groups and forums." Kim sighed. "In fact, I followed some of the discussions. They weren't pretty."

Later that afternoon he sent me links to some of those pages. For example, on 5 January Emrah Gunyuzlu had written: "Where are the Jews assembling? And; are there

37

any organizations joining the Palestinians? Looking forward to Thursday!"[6]

Many posts were just informative and supportive, but others were more ugly. That same day Ayan Hussaini wrote: "i swear hitler showed them fuckers what time it was ... !! look at them killing people like is nothing ... !! and people say osama and sadam was heartless ... No one cant get low as them fucking jews ... !! there just haters ... muslims are strong people and inshalla allah will help them trough this ... All we can do is pray for them!!" [sic].

Other posts were even more portentous, like this 7 January one from Ibrahim Battakh: "What the fuck are you arguing about? Find out where a Jew lives and then you can talk. We gather people and find the Jews, damn it!!"

Revoltingly, on 7 January Asad Ahmad wrote: "Sad, that is all I am saying. Israel and the rest of the Jewish bastards can burn in Hell. People hate Hitler, and so do I. But not because of his cruelty, but because he did not get them all!!"

These posts, quite typical of the discussion, genuinely surprised me. Without doubt, Kim was right: the riots had been planned, and they were to be directed against Jews. This realization added to my growing astonishment. Surely

---

6. One such thread, called "Opprør mot Israel" (Rebellion Against Israel), was here: http://www.facebook.com/event.php?sid=b553c1f16885b88e 33485ff976dc8d98&eid=42178237601#/wall.php?id=42178237601&pa ge=14&hash=6032c0613698a0c254be047f9f37e1b5. All the comments I have quoted were taken from this page, accessed January 9, 2009. (The page has since been removed.)

no one following this thread could have failed to notice what was brewing.

But on this Friday morning few in the media seemed aware of the gravity of the situation. Everybody seemed shocked by the riots' intensity, but few grasped their character. Generally, appearing in various media, sociologists and politicians made excuses for the angry youth, offering superficial talk about failed integration and social exclusion of young Muslims. Of course, these factors do partly explain why the flames were ignited that night, but in no way whatsoever do they excuse anti-Jewish hate crimes.

As for the Palestinian support groups, they chose not to condemn the attacks, although, for the record, some of them publicly "recommended" nonviolence. Olaf Svorstøl, the leader of the Norwegian Coalition for Palestine (Fellesutvalget for Palestina), told *Aftenposten*, "We do not want to judge those who chose other kinds of actions. Siv Jensen's provocations made people angry. We do not distinguish between worthy and unworthy demonstrations." Svorstøl said that the pro-Israeli crowd was largely to blame for the riots and the violence.

I admit that I have a problem with such irresponsibility.

How did the radical Left respond? I expected little from the left-wing party Rødt (Red, formerly RV) or the leftist daily, *Klassekampen*. Both sprang out of the Maoist AKP (ml) party in the 1970s and for more than 30 years now have been promoting their skewed perspective that national liberation struggles are an anti-imperialist force. In earlier years their members strongly supported such movements in Vietnam, Palestine, and Afghanistan. Later, after Pol Pot, Enver Hoxha, and Mao Tse-Tung lost their allure, these leftists readily embraced the new "anti-imperialism" represented by the mujahideen and the ayatollahs; some, like Lena Larsen and Trond Ali Lindstad, even converted to Islam. Similar political ideals and aims continue today, particularly in a relentless anti-Americanism and anti-Zionism.

One party encompassed by Rødt is the small Trotskyite group Internasjonale Sosialister (connected to Tony Cliff's Socialist Workers Party). On the subject of nationalism, the IS is usually far more reasonable than the Maoists, but they nonetheless nurture a particular hatred for Zionism. Like the SWP in Great Britain, the IS staunchly opposes "Israeli aggression" and supports "the resistance": in an earlier demo, their placards read, "Boycott Israel, not Hamas."

In the 3 January issue of *Klassekampen* the veteran RV/Rødt-member Trond Andresen asserted that Israelis are mentally ill: that they lack empathy for other peoples. According to Andresen, it is now time to tell Jews that "many in your ethnic group have a serious empathy problem." In 2004, similar dehumanizing characterizations had led RV to exclude Hans Olav Brendberg, another long-standing member, from the party.[7] Despite the commotion

---

7.  Kjetil Simonsen briefly discusses this incident in his essay, "Anti-Semitism in the Socialist Tradition," *Communalism* 11 (August 2007).

the exclusion of Brendberg caused at the time, the editors of *Klassekampen* continue publishing such diatribes.

If the Maoist left performed as expected, how did the libertarian Left respond to the riots? Around the world anarchists and autonomists had decried the "massacres in Gaza," often carelessly adopting anti-Zionist rhetoric about defending "the resistance" against "Israeli aggression." Norwegian left-libertarians were no exception.

Norwegian anarchists and autonomists are basically "organized" around Blitz, an alternative social center that emerged from squats more than 25 years ago. This "self-managed youth center" has been, and continues to be, an important alternative scene in Oslo's subcultural landscape. As an antifascist, I've often sided with Blitz in fighting xenophobic and right-wing tendencies, and I have been connected to its music scene as well. Through Blitz and Anti-Fascist Action, I have participated in mobilizations against neo-Nazis and other fascists in Sweden, Germany, and Denmark as well as Norway: several times I've engaged in street fighting. Such mobilizations were more than necessary.

But the general political line of the Blitz milieu has always been highly problematic – it lacks any *positive ideology whatsoever.* Instead, Blitz expresses only fragments of anarchist, syndicalist, Maoist, and feminist ideas, in support of "youth rebellion" and "struggles for liberation."

This eclecticism is normally not a problem, simply because no one outside Blitz – and few within the scene

– takes it seriously as a political alternative. But on this Friday, the limitations of Blitz's "politics" were exposed.

On Thursday Blitz had announced on its website that it "supports and welcomes the rebels and looks forward to participating in future struggles against the occupation of Palestine." Now friends in the milieu told me that people from Blitz had been actively involved in the protests; I wondered what they would make of the anti-Jewish attacks. I knew Blitz activists had been present when Jan Thomas's beauty salon was struck – I assumed they would want to distance themselves from anti-Semitism and hate crimes. But when I visited its website, I found that Blitz made no such confession.

Instead, they challenged media portrayals of the riots as "nonpolitical mob actions." *No*, they asserted, the riots had indeed been political. And further: "A rebellion does not happen simply because someone encourages it – there are always underlying reasons. No matter where or when, Blitz will always support youth when they rebel."[8]

When I read that last sentence, I went numb.

*No matter where or when.*

---

8    Blitz removed this statement a few days after the riots, but *never excused it*. I add it here (in Norwegian) because it explains how Blitz activists would act on Saturday: "Opprør skjer ikke fordi noen oppfordrer til det, det er alltid en bakenforliggende årsak. Blitz vil for alltid støtte ungdomsopprør der det skjer, når det skjer." (http://www.blitz.no. Accessed 11 January.)

I could hardly believe it. In just a few sentences, all the conventional prejudices against Blitz – that they are just mindless protestors looking for clashes with the authorities – seemed confirmed. I was so disappointed.

*Always support youth when they rebel.*

Really? Regardless of what they rebel against? Regardless of what they are fighting for? Was this really what they advocated? Was Blitz rationalizing participation in anti-Jewish riots through a blind adherence to "youth rebellion"?

A group that gives blanket support to "youth rebellion" will be bound to give its support all causes that have that particular characteristic. But some "youth rebellions" may be in contradiction to the group's other ideals. Historically, many youth movements have been reactionary and many riots have favored the privileged. Unfortunately, neither the word "youth" nor "rebellion" possesses any magical qualities.

If social radicalism is mistaken for "rebelliousness" or even simply for "rioting," there is indeed very little "Left" in it. In fact, such criteria make it impossible for us to distinguish between, say, the New York Draft Riots and the Stonewall Riots. Unless we have a reliable ethical compass and firm political principles, radical actions can easily serve reactionary political ends.

Blitz's statement revealed that its radicals have no principles at all.

What happened to ideals of "social liberation," "antiracism," and "solidarity"? Autonomists and anarchists claim such ideals as their own, and they have defended them over and over again. Was Blitz really ready to abandon everything it had claimed to fight for, just for the thrill of fighting some cops and smashing some windowpanes?

"The kids are losing their minds," goes the catchy Ramones tune, and I was ready to agree. It's one thing to commit an embarrassing mistake, in the heat of a moment, amid a youth scene that is far from uniform politically. But to rationalize it afterward and try to make it into a political statement is something entirely different.

That night I went out to meet Kim. Over a few beers at a party, we shared our thoughts about the war, the protests, the media, and the reactions from the Left. As we watched the young punks at the party, with all their regalia, their dreadlocks, and their good intentions, excited by the prospects of new clashes with the police, I admit I felt sad, and genuinely scared. Punk recklessness had shown its dark side.

"What they want, I don't know. *They're all revved up and ready to go.*"

A new, broader demonstration against Israel's warfare on the Gaza strip had been announced for the next afternoon, Saturday. I had a nagging fear that it would bring more worms out of the woodwork.

# *Wonderful, Second Time Around*

Understanding now that Thursday's riots had been planned, and having observed the Left's vapid responses, I was anxious about what would happen at today's demonstration.

Posters had been announcing it for a week – it was to take place at the parliament square at two o'clock. The massive press coverage would ensure a large turnout. It was to be the major mobilization of all forces in support of the Palestinian struggle, from punks and revolutionaries to religious leaders and politicians – everyone would be there. What would the afternoon bring?

I made an appointment with Peter, an old friend who'd helped run a radical bookstore in Porsgrunn in the mid-1990s. He was also a competent photographer – a skill that might come in handy. As we headed downtown, he told me about his own experience at Thursday's demonstrations – he had overheard people yelling "Jewish pigs" and "Freemasons" at the pro-Israeli crowd.

We arrived at the square a little before two. There was no riot fence this time, and few police were visible. Many people were already there.

As I was about to enter the crowd, an elegant, elderly woman in a large fur coat handed me a flyer written by Grandmothers for Peace, demanding an end to "Israeli aggression."

Peter and I wandered around, talking to friends and acquaintances we met. More people turned up, many from immigrant organizations. Sizable contingents of socialists of all strands arrived, waving their red flags: The youth organizations were particularly visible, but many older people showed up too. Israel seems to be one of the few issues that can pry regular party members out of their chairs these days.

I even bumped into Kristin Halvorsen, the leader of Socialist Left Party and the current finance minister. A few years ago, just when this "Red-Green" coalition government was forming, she was heavily criticized for calling for a boycott of Israeli products. This had not deterred her from supporting this cause publicly today: When I passed her, she was standing close to a small placard saying "The Greatest Axes of Evil: USA and Israel"[9]

We looked at the banners and symbols. A nearby placard read "The Occupant Power Israel: The Greatest Threat to World Peace," while another lumped together all the evils:

---

9. I later saw a published photo of this, http://www.dagsavisen.no/innenriks/article391177.ece?pageNum=5&status=showall.

"UN/USA/Israel on a Murder Raid; Thieves, Bandits – Enough is enough!"

Hatred of Israel seethed on the placards and banners – indeed, it was palpable in the very ambience. But the demonstration was quiet. The people from Blitz seemed particularly circumspect. They arrived a little late, as they had been halted en route by police, who arrested – for no good reasons – one of their most prominent activists, Stein Lillevolden.

I was now behind the speakers' platform, and I craned my neck to read some of the banners hanging there. Suddenly one of the demo's guards pushed me aside. He was clearing the way for a group of some ten children to pass. The kids were taken up to the platform, to pose before the banners. All were draped in white cloth that was stained by artificial blood, and they duly carried keffiyehs. An emphasis on victimized children had been part of the media coverage ever since the first bombs fell, and it had made the numerous denunciations of Israelis as "child murderers" seem legitimate. But such charges should not be made lightly.

In fact, the use of this imagery should concern us. Don't journalists know that the Blood Libel has haunted Jews ever since the Middle Ages? It has certainly undergone variations from an anti-Judaic, to an anti-Semitic, and now to an anti-Israeli form, but labeling Jews as "child murderers" has been a *constant* theme in anti-Jewish propaganda ever since the twelfth century!

In my view, nowadays this imagery is used cynically, *precisely because* of its strong resonance in popular imagination.

Many of the banners at Saturday's demonstration cast Israelis as deliberate "child murderers." One banner simply read, "Stop the murder of children," as if the conflict in Gaza was about whether children should be killed. Others condemned "Israeli terror." None of them, not one, criticized the "resistance movement," Hamas.

As the speakers began, Peter and I drifted off to the side.

We wanted to *watch* the rally, not actually *join* it, so we strolled up Karl Johan, through Castle Park, and sat down in a bookstore-café in the House of Literature, where we had coffee. From this corner of the park, overlooking the entrance to the Israeli embassy, we got a splendid view of the proceedings.

The original plan had been that the speakers would have their say, and then the demonstrators would march to the Israeli embassy. But that morning the organizers had apparently agreed just to keep the demonstration in front of the parliament and go no further. Perhaps they feared a repetition or even an escalation of the Thursday riots – that would have been tactically unwise, as anti-Israeli sentiments could then lose public support.

Once the speakers were finished, a representative of a large Norwegian trade union (the LO) took the microphone to announce the decision. But before he could finish, Basim Ghozlan, a prominent spokesperson from the Islamic Union, interrupted him and said that those who wished to would indeed go to the embassy. After some confusion, most of the demonstrators – in fact, thousands – joined the march. The "blood-stained" children were placed at the forefront. All began striding up Karl Johan Street.

As they passed before Peter and me, we were struck by both their numbers and their energy. We had brought our coffee cups outside and watched from the stairs. The march moved steadily past us and then assembled in front of the embassy. It had grown in size, for sure, and was far more fervent.

The demonstrators chanted the usual anti-Israeli slogans and seemed moderate – whatever that means in this context. But then a new, large group arrived, and from them I heard the unmistakable "Al *Mawt al-Yahud*": Death to the Jews. This call was repeated many times, with small variations, and every time the crowd responded, *Allahu Akbar* – God is great.

The large size of the new contingent, and its unconcealed hatred of Jews, was appalling. Nobody seemed concerned.

"So this is what reaction looks like," I said to Peter in amazement.

At the police line, tension was growing. The protesters were hurling rocks and fireworks at the embassy and at the police, who kept a low profile. Curiously, as the barrage got rougher, the "blood-stained" mascots were placed in between the police and the militant protesters. (Afterward this move would meet with severe criticism in the media: the organizers would be accused of using the children as human shields.[10])

As the marchers chanted, the front line pushed closer to the embassy. Fireworks sputtered profusely from the crowd. Someone climbed a lamppost and raised the Palestinian flag, and the crowd cheered; others burned the Israeli flag, and they cheered wildly.

One of the popular slogans was "Stop the aggression: Shut down the embassy." At first I found it amusingly ironic, as one of the demonstration's main demands was for Israel to recognize Hamas and enter into negotiations with this "resistance movement." But then the slogan was twisted into "Blow up the embassy" (the Norwegian words *Steng* and *Spreng* sound similar), and it was no longer funny. Later someone told me they had even heard people shout, "Gas the embassy."

Again, the demonstration was not only pro-Palestinian but distinctly anti-Israeli. Perhaps some or even many did not share the extreme viewpoints of the visible and vocal anti-Jewish elements, but if so, they did nothing to distance themselves. People shouted condemnations of everything Israeli, Zionist, or Jewish. Many even used overt Nazi analogies. One protester carried a placard made in the colors of the Israeli flag, where skull and crossbones had replaced the Magen David; the caption read "Fascist state."

10. See http://www.dagbladet.no/2009/01/11/nyheter/innenriks/ demonstrasjon/4332348/.

Another banner simply said "Israel," in large blood-red letters; the S was made as a swastika. Still another placard equated Ehud Olmert with Adolf Hitler.

Some young Somali women – masked behind hijabs and keffiyehs – carried even more eccentric placards. One read, "Judes. The chosen people. A shame for humanity!" [*sic*]. Another: "SionJews. The blood is flowing. Soon comes Mehdi with friends" [*sic*]. None of the demonstrators seemed to have any problems with Israeli-Nazi analogies or anti-Jewish eschatology.

Such placards and slogans stunned me. *Why did none of the guards, participants, or organizers stop these obvious excesses?* The placards and banners were clearly visible. I'm sure many of the 75 or more demonstration guards spoke Arabic and understood the slogans' significance. Why did not Basim Ghozlan stop them? What about Line Khateeb from Palestinian Committee?

Another placard, carried by a man of about 40, now attracted our attention. It read, "*Hayber, Hayber ya Yehud.*" Surmising that *yehud* meant "Jews," we wondered what the other words meant.

"I have to take some photos," Peter called back to me, descending the stairs. Then he went over to the man and asked him directly what the placard said.

"I don't now how to translate it correctly," the man replied.

"But it's about Jews. 'Yehud' means Jews, doesn't it?"

"No, no, it's not that, but … I don't know Norwegian very well. I'm sorry."

"But then why are you carrying this placard?"

"Because it calls for peace in the Middle East. That's what it means."

Peter took some photos and came back up the stairs and joined me where I was in the background, keeping my distance. Then a large group got militant and started pushing toward the police barricade. The police hung back, but right in front of us they arrested a protester, perhaps 35 years old with a blond beard. During his arrest, he kept telling one of the officers, who had a darker complexion than the rest, that he was on "the wrong side."

Peter and I went back into the bookstore-café. I bought a new book by Gilles Kepel, and then we decided to head over to Peter's place. It was now 16.45, and we were both hungry. As we drifted away, police horses were moving their lines closer, narrowing and concentrating the demonstration. At the same time several guards were taking off their yellow vests, and we overheard them saying to protesters and bystanders that the allotted time for the demonstration was over. This was not a good sign, as the crowd seemed as pugnacious as ever.

But we'd seen enough.

Walking toward Pilestredet, Peter took some photos of windowpanes. With big letters, someone had tagged them with "Kill the Zionists."

We went into a grocery store to find something quick to eat. When we came back out, we smelled CS gas, a clear indication that police were charging the demonstration. Even though we were far from the embassy by now, the gas strongly irritated our faces and we hurried on. Arriving at Peter's place, we eagerly turned on the TV to hear the latest. Devouring our nan-pizzas, we saw that the police action had unleashed scattered rioting, with a series of attacks on the all-too-familiar targets for the mob's anger.

We followed the news the rest of the evening – and got more and more of a disturbing picture. Demonstrations in all corners of Europe, we saw, had degenerated into violent clashes with police, and symbols of alleged Jewish power had been destroyed. McDonald's and Starbucks in particular had been targeted, we learned. In Oslo some five McDonald's restaurants were attacked, some totally smashed, while surprised families were evacuated into the basement. Apart from the embassy, McDonald's restaurants were the main targets of the angry mob.

Why?

For the past week a rumor had been spreading that McDonald's was a Jewish enterprise, providing money for the Israeli war effort. At the demonstration earlier that day, some friends had told us about a text message that they'd received. Apparently, a lot of people had received it: "McDonald's has decided that everything they earn on Saturday will be sent to Israel… Help us make sure that they don't earn anything this Saturday! And forward this message!"

Peter and I looked at each other in amazement, then went online to find out more. I checked the Facebook pages, and sure enough, a message posted on 5 January, from Ibrar Ahmad, read: "As you surely know, McDonalds, Burger King, etc. are owned by Jews. So, this coming Saturday, McDonalds will send all the money they earn to Israel. That will give them more money so they will be capable of killing several thousands more of the innocent children in Gaza. If you support Gaza, you should boycott McDonalds. *Do it for the innocent, poor, civilian, human beings in Palestine*. Forward this message to everyone you know, and less people will die!!!!"

"How is that possible?" Peter shook his head in disbelief. "I mean, this has been discredited since I don't know when."

I was equally baffled.

We'd known about the text message but had not thought it would have such repercussions. We'd even giggled about it. But we both knew how easily people come to accept such rumors.

After all, a rumor like the one about McDonald's fits hand in glove with the old stereotypical "moneyed Jew" or delusions about "Jewish capital." Jews are greedy and cunning, these rumors say, controlling the world through hidden commercial networks.

So the momentous implications of the McDonald's rumor should not be underestimated. Ever since the Middle Ages, attacks on Jews and Jewish property have been instigated by vicious rumors that both confirmed and fueled ingrained popular prejudices. Usually these rumors had only faint bases in truth, but that did not hamper their continued persistence in legitimizing "spontaneous" attacks on Jews.

Later, at the end of the nineteenth century, similar rumor-mongering would ignite pogroms in Eastern Europe and Russia.

This weekend showed to the full that anti-Semitic prejudices still have a mobilizing potential, even here in Oslo.

In my view, the stunning success of that unfounded rumor proves just how potent anti-Semitism still is – precisely because it subcurrents in our culture, both in Europe and in the Arab world.

Beyond their sheer stupidity, the extent to which these rumors resonate with age-old anti-Semitic prejudices and practices should be cause for alarm. Not only do they perpetuate the myth of omnipotent "Jewish capital," they open the door to conspiracy theories. This evening would also display the vitality of another ancient myth: Freemasonry as a Jewish conspiracy.

Anti-Freemasonry has old roots in the Christian tradition, particularly as a reaction to the Great French Revolution of 1789. The Freemasons, it was believed, were revolutionaries and cosmopolitans who worked to undermine the established order; their plotting had toppled the *ancien régime*. Anti-Freemasonry is often connected to anti-Semitic conspiracism.

The Hamas Charter condemns Freemasonry as a "secret society" that was founded as a part of the alleged Zionist plot to control the world. Hitler's *Mein Kampf* presents the same view. This is not a coincidence: both base much of their analysis on the notorious forgery *Protocols of the Elders of Zion*. Published a few years before the outbreak of the Russian Revolution of 1905, agents of the Okhrana had authored this document in order to channel popular discontent against the Jews, to discredit them and thereby legitimize their repression. The tsarist secret police knew how powerful such a document could be, consciously crafting it upon the prejudices of the day.

These delusions have been successfully exported to the worldview of many Islamists. Indeed, Hamas blames the Jews for instigating just about every revolution and war that has occurred in history. According to the Hamas Charter, Jews were "behind the French Revolution, the Communist revolution and most of the revolutions we heard and hear about, here and there." And further, "There is no war going on anywhere, without having their finger in it." Despite the dismal history of the last century, some still believe in a Jewish world conspiracy.

As Peter and I watched the news, we saw that for some, holding this crazy idea was not sufficient; it had to be put into action as well. Several protesters had approached a journalist. "Come with us!" they said, promising that he would witness something he "had never seen before."

"The building of the Freemasons! *Go! Go! Go!*" we heard from off camera, on the video clip.

"Why?" asked the journalist.

"The Freemasons," was the short reply.

"Yes, but *why*?" the journalist asked.

"Because they're motherfuckers. They rule the world!"[11]

At the Masonic building, protesters threw rocks and bottles at the windows. After several minutes and many attempts, they broke a window, and someone threw in fireworks, which exploded inside. I found out later that while this was happening, some 200 children were inside the building, terrified by the attack. As it happens, the Masonic Lodge was holding its annual Christmas tree party that day.

As if attacks on delusory symbols of "Jewish power" were not troubling enough, there were also several attacks on alleged Jews that night.

"We were asked to hunt Jews," said a 12-year-old kid who had taken part in the ensuing riots. Five older youths had led the crowd through the streets, and then told them what to attack, as drum players from Blitz accompanied them. According to the kid, the youths "beat up a man who wanted to stop them from rampaging his store. First someone cried out that he was a Jew, then they hit him in turn, one hit him with the elbow in the neck. Everyone I saw attack him kicked and hit him in the head in order to damage him as severely as possible."[12]

Then the kids were asked to go up to Blindern (the university area) "to hunt Jews." To understand the gravity

---

11. See http://www.abcnyheter.no/node/81209.
12. See http://www.dagbladet.no/2009/01/11/nyheter/2400/innenriks/oslo/tyveri/4324990/.

of this demand, my readers should know that both on Thursday and on Saturday, police had confiscated knives, Molotov cocktails, and clubs.

Fortunately, as far as I can tell, they didn't find anyone.

Actually, it probably would have been hard for these mobs to find Jews in Oslo.

After all, only some 1,100 live there, and apart from well-known public figures like Jo Benkow, Anne Sender, and the late Berthold Grünfeld, they are largely indistinguishable from the general population. Jews were only allowed into the Norwegian Kingdom in 1851; in the following decades many immigrated from the East, particularly Lithuania; their descendants have deep roots here. Although a horrifying proportion of Norway's Jewish population perished in death camps during World War II, Jews have been an integral to Norwegian culture and a source of considerable enrichment. It would therefore not be easy for these mobs to find targets for their rage.

But suppose their targets had been discernable. Suppose they were forced to wear a yellow Magen David – what would have been the result? Having personally felt the rage Thursday night, I shudder to think.

In July 2006, after several frightening episodes, Oslo's Jewish Community warned its members against publicly wearing yarmulkes or other symbols of Jewish identity. The following September their synagogue was attacked with automatic weapons. Around that time Norwegian police reported that the Algerian Islamist GSPC (Groupe Salafiste pour la Prédication et le Combat) also was planning attacks on this synagogue in Oslo.

Although this identification of all Jews with the state of Israel may perhaps be recent in Norway, it is not particularly new elsewhere. After the Six-Day War in 1967, the Jordanian minister for social affairs, Emile Algohri, said, "It is our firm belief that there is no difference at all between Jews and Zionists. All Jews are Zionists and all Zionists are Jews, and anyone who thinks otherwise is not thinking logically. We consider world Jewry our adversary and enemy, as we do imperialism and all the pro-Jewish powers."

Now in January 2009, the Jewish kindergarten in Oslo will report that they do not dare let their children play outdoors. Why? During the war, Hamas declared that Jewish institutions and Jews all over the world are target for their revenge. Not only are all Jews absurdly held responsible for whatever Israeli politicians do: so are their children.

We saw more examples of how protest against Israeli policy is transposed into a general hatred of Jews, indeed becomes indistinguishable from it. Another video from Saturday afternoon showed protesters clashing with the police.[13]

---

13. See http://www.liveleak.com/view?i=25d_1231552669. My translation (I could not decipher the last few words in Arabic of the young woman's speech).

One defiantly asks a policeman, "*Who* are you protecting?" and "*What* are you protecting?" then exclaims "Al *Mawt al Yahud!*" several times. Others accompany him with cries of "Jews!" and "Child murderers!"

In the same video a journalist asks a young woman, "What do you think about what you are witnessing here today?" Her reply is telling: "There is much chaos, and many big problems, but I actually think that – well, violence doesn't solve anything in this world – but you see that young children, young boys stand up for their own religion, you see ..." A passerby crying "Free Palestine" interrupts, and she comments, "Exactly, there you got it." Continuing her train of thought, she says: "Israel does shitty things to Muslim children and innocent youths, to women who have done nothing, to children who have not yet lived their life, you see. Of course, that makes blood rush to the head, and all children are fighting, all children run amok, all children lose control. I only say this: Jihad! God is Great!" to the applause of her friends.

Hearing her speak this way in front of these rebellious youth, I couldn't help wondering how many of the underage casualties in Gaza had been actual combatants. After all, much of the sympathy for the Palestinian cause is fed by the images of from the Intifada, in which rebellious youth confront the Israeli army with only stones, slings, and pellets.

Peter and I discussed this powerful symbol of youth radicalism.

Somewhere he still had a worn keffiyeh, from the days of the First Intifada, and I reminisced that I had once adored these very images when I first became radicalized in the early 1990s: Young people have been the symbol of the two Intifadas.

Such images presented an attractive version of David and Goliath, adding youthful heroism to the Palestinian cause. Given basic training, an AK-47, or perhaps an RPG, the fearless kids might well take on the Israeli army in combat, however unfair the odds.

But today the images coming from Hamas and its youth organizations are far grimmer: young soldiers and very young children posing as soldiers or suicide bombers. Hamas has posted videos showing that women too prepare for and fulfill their "martyrdom."

On 29 February 2008 Fathi Hammad, a member of the Palestinian Legislative Council, stated on the Hamas-run Al-Aqsa TV, "For the Palestinian people death has become an industry at which women excel, and so do all the people on this land. The elderly excel at this, and so do the mujahideen and the children." And further, "This is why they have formed human shields of the women, the children, the elderly, and the mujahideen in order to challenge the Zionist bombing machine. It is as if they were saying to the Zionist enemy: 'We desire death as you desire life.'"

If only for these reasons, the remarks of the young woman protesting in Oslo completely miss the picture. But she put words to conceptions that are widely held.

In condemning support for Israel as "un-Christian," Bishop Stålsett has said, "saving civilian lives must take a higher priority than tactical and strategic concerns." Civilian victims are lamentable, but counting them in a conflict like this never is easy. It cuts both ways. I remember well how Basim Ghozlan, back in 2004, defended suicide bombers, as it stirred some discussion in Norway. Seemingly in line with Yussuf al-Quaradawi, Ghozlan wrote, "Most people seem to think civilians are the ones wearing ordinary clothes, while soldiers wear army uniforms. Palestinians know that all Israeli citizens are militants." And further, "They are occupiers, whatever clothes they are wearing. Most Palestinians therefore do not consider the victims of suicide actions to be 'innocent civilians.'"

Taken together, these statements from Ghozlan and the young woman reflect a skewed notion of who is "civilian" and who is a "combatant." Starkly contrasting standards are used when judging Israelis or Jews on the one hand, and Palestinians and Muslims on the other. Certainly modern asymmetrical warfare shakes our common conceptions of perpetrator and victim. Still, when wanton reprisals or "collective punishment" is decried, a measure of consistency should be expected: A wrong does not become a right when the other party commits it.

For others, such distinctions between civilians and combatants are obviously not at all important. In the same video an older man tries to stop the crowd's rampage. His reward is to be pushed from behind and suffer several blows to his head, to cries of "al Jihad."

Peter and I still wanted to clarify the meaning of *"Hayber, Hayber ya Yehud,"* so we sat down to trawl it on the Internet search engines. First our searches bore no results. Then we found out that the slogan is a linguistic twist of a more common Arabic slogan that has been chanted at anti-Israeli protests for many years now. The whole slogan goes like this: *"Khaybar, Khaybar ya Yahud, jaysh Muhammad sauf ya'ud."*[14] A literal translation would be "Khaybar, Khaybar, O you Jews, the army of Muhammad shall return."

But what does that mean? As we read more, we found that "Khaybar" is the name of an oasis that once housed the largest Jewish settlement in the Arabian Peninsula. In 629 CE, in a famous battle there, Muhammad and his followers defeated the Jews. A few years later the Jewish population was expelled from the whole area, and since then the conquest of Khaybar has been remembered as the event that placed *dhimmis* (non-Muslims, like Jews) under Muslim rule.

Many Islamists see Israel as a perpetual affront simply for existing as a separate political entity in traditional Muslim land, in what should be part of *Dar al-Islam*. Like the fortresses of Khaybar, they say when they chant this slogan, Israel must be vanquished.

---

14. On 22 January the Norwegian organization With Israel for Peace posted pictures from the 8 January counterdemonstration, revealing that the slogan was present even there. See http://miff.no/nyheter/2009/01/22M assakreTruslerMotJoederIOslo.html.

Khaybar evidently carries a very powerful symbolism. We found out that a new Iranian-produced assault rifle is named Khaybar (KH-2002). Khaybar-1 and Khaybar-2 are also the names Hezbollah chose for the rockets they fired on Israel in 2006. And Khaybar is also an international point of reference for Islamists. When Amrozi bin Nurhasin, the Bali bomber, entered the courtroom on the day he was sentenced, he reportedly shouted: "Jews, remember Khaybar. The army of Muhammad is coming back to defeat you."

The significance of this slogan, then, must not be underestimated.

As midnight approached, it was time for me to go home. I tried to think of something to put on to make a visible political statement, but all my ideas seemed tacky, so I went into the night. The city was calm.

Another darkness followed me home that night: I couldn't help thinking about the conversation between Peter and the placard-bearer.

"Peace in the Middle East." Yeah, right.

The crazy thing is that, within the anti-Semitic worldview, the slogan could make sense as a peace statement. Just defeat the Jews, and there will be no more war against them. Get rid of them all – find a "final solution" – and peace will come to the Middle East. Its resemblances to messages from the last century may be troubling to Europeans, but the slogan is today echoed in Gaza and the West Bank and in other Arab countries, by many imams and political leaders. According to former Iranian president Hashemi Rafsanjani, "The everlasting struggle between Ishmael and Isaac cannot cease until one or the other is utterly vanquished." After all, "every problem in our region can be traced to this single dilemma: the occupation of Dar al-Islam by Jewish infidels or Western imperialists." Palestine therefore becomes a unique focal point for Islamists, who cynically use it for its symbolic value in their struggle against Jews and the West.

Some may interpret the slogan as a call to "free Palestine," to regain Dar al-Islam and throw all Jews into the sea, to rid the world of a Jewish cabal, or some other specious reason. Regardless of its interpretation, this slogan – "*Khaybar, Khaybar ya Yahud*" – cannot represent anything but a purely irrational hate politics.

Approaching the apartment that was my home for a few turbulent days, I saw that on a wall somebody had scribbled, "No Jews."

# *Paint it Black*

When I awoke on Sunday morning, I felt like I had a hangover, even though I hadn't been drinking.

I started collecting my thoughts.

The events I had witnessed were not aberrations, I said to myself. The protests had uncovered sinister underlying sentiments. It was on this morning that I concluded that I had witnessed anti-Jewish riots, and nothing else.

For the next few hours I paced restlessly between the windows, the sofa, and the computer. How could they have happened? As far as I can judge, these were the largest anti-Jewish riots in Norwegian history. Even before and during World War II, when anti-Semitic prejudices were strong, public policies were discriminatory, and the Nazified State Police efficiently confiscated Jewish property and deported Jews on that despicable slave ship SS *Donau* – even then, Norway had not seen anti-Jewish outbursts of this scale. This country had no previous history of wanton anti-Jewish mass violence.

This weekend Norway crossed a threshold. No euphemism can conceal it. And no rationalization or justification can redeem it.

And I was there.

Feeling small and powerless, I spent most of Sunday surfing the Internet, trying to grasp the extent of the weekend's riots.

Evidently they were not confined to Oslo: public protests took place in more than 30 Norwegian cities. Several of these protests, I was later told, tolerated anti-Jewish elements of the type I had witnessed in Oslo (some were apparently even displaying Nazi symbols.) About 3,000 people had gathered in Trondheim to decry Israel's war on Hamas. This city, located in the middle of Norway, has a strong pro-Palestinian sentiment. In the autumn of 2005 its county government decreed an official boycott of Israeli goods, and national liberation movements have gained significant support from left-wing parties, trade unions, and autonomists in this region.

In the most disturbing episode so far, the teachers of a class of sixth-grade pupils canceled the annual trip to Trondheim's synagogue, where the widow of Julius Paltiel, an Auschwitz survivor, was to take the children around and teach them about the Holocaust and Judaism. The trip was canceled because the visit would "generate aggression" among the pupils. When the Jewish Museum in Oslo recently sent out invitations to schools for such trips, one teacher replied that he would visit the museum only "when Palestine was liberated."

In a speech in Tromsø, the city's mayor, Arild Hausberg from the Labor party, flippantly compared the Gaza "resistance" to the Warsaw ghetto uprising of 1943. The doctor Mads Gilbert repeated this comparison several times and also likened the bombing raids on Gaza to the bombing of Dresden, which, although imprecise, was a far less distasteful comparison. These deceptive assertions quickly entered the public imagination as "truths."

On that last Thursday all trains had been stopped for two minutes, while an announcement came over the loudspeakers: the unionized locomotive drivers in Norway had called a rare political general strike "in support for Gaza." Several major trade unions have called for boycott of Israeli products, and there has even been a campaign to boycott Israeli artists and academics. Israel indeed "generates aggression" among the Norwegian public.

I still had not fully recovered from my experience of the preceding days. It all seemed so surreal. And that afternoon, as I was drinking coffee, trying not to feel paralyzed, I wondered what had happened in Norway's neighboring countries. How had events played out there?

I surfed the Net. Had it gone this far, say, in Sweden?

In several respects: Yes, absolutely.

A major survey in 2005 revealed widespread anti-Semitism in Sweden.[15] Out of a sample of 3,000 Swedes aged

---

15. Henrik Bachner and Jonas Ring, *Antisemitiska attityder och föreställningar i Sverige* (Stockholm: Forum för levande historia, 2005).

16 to 75, fully 41 percent harbored anti-Semitic views: 5 percent were full-fledged anti-Semites. 26 percent believed that Israel dealt with the Palestinians more or less as the Nazis had dealt with the Jews, and the same percentage thought the Israelis operated according to the biblical concept of "an eye for eye." Twenty-five percent would not consider a Jewish prime minister to be acceptable. I am afraid that these attitudes have not improved over the last four years.

Sweden is the home of several relatively significant radical nationalist parties and outright neo-Nazi groups. Like the National Socialist Front, they mostly advance traditional anti-Semitism. Neo-Nazis have repeatedly protested the Gaza offensive with swastikas and keffiyehs.

Sweden have also seen an ugly upsurge of anti-Semitic hate attacks since the "Second Intifada." On 18 April 2002, a rally held in Stockholm to protest anti-Semitism and Islamophobia was stormed. The attackers, mostly of immigrant origin, physically attacked participants, destroyed placards, and shouted "Jewish swine!" and "*Allahu Akbar!*" Many of those in the rally, including some Holocaust survivors, suffered injury and shock during the 15 minutes before the police intervened.

Certain intellectuals found this event not so grave. In 2003 the late Jan Samuelsson, a professor of comparative religion, said Arab and Muslim anti-Semitism in Sweden is "understandable, reasonable, and justified."

Lately such "understandable, reasonable, and justified" hatred has appeared in the suburbs of Malmø, where pro-

Israeli demonstrations have been attacked and individuals harassed. Early in January, incendiaries attacked the synagogue in nearby Helsingborg. The chapel of the Jewish cemetery in Malmö was also attacked twice with petrol bombs. A certain Dan Park expressed himself with subtle and profound artistry: outside the cemetery he left cans illustrated with a Magen David and the label "Zyklon B."

Other anti-Semites, like Ahmed Rami, are less subtle. Starting in the 1980s this Holocaust denier ran a radio station called *Radio Islam*, wherein he consistently attacked Jews, Israel, and its supporters. After numerous complaints over several years, the authorities shut the station down, and he now spreads his hate message online.

Recent demonstrations in Sweden, organized by well-meaning Social Democrats, have seen the green and yellow flags of the various jihadist movements raised; here too naïve supporters of "peace" blend seamlessly with intransigent enemies of "Zionism." And here too, videos show that crowds of protesters carrying Palestinian flags burned Israeli flags, to cries of "*Allahu Akbar*" and "Death to Israel."

With some notable exceptions, the majority of anarchists and autonomists in Sweden are distinctly anti-Israeli. In the last five years one clandestine network – Global Intifada – has attained notoriety for radical actions against Israel, the United States, and countries that participate in the war in Iraq.

This weekend, at one of the large rallies in Stockholm, the high-profile libertarian socialist Andreas Malm (who had earlier voiced support for Hezbollah) welcomed the "Palestinian revolution." As I considered that Islamists now dominate Gaza – and how Hamas was actually preparing to introduce a strict Sharia penal code there (including floggings, mutilations, and crucifixions!), primarily directed toward their fellow Arabs in Palestine – Malm's statements sent chills down my spine. Hamas was *never* a liberatory force. Why pretend that it is?

Again, I asked myself: Why do calls for national liberation *always* tend to replace more fundamental calls for social liberation? And why does that agenda always conceal the social, cultural and political conflicts *within* a nation? Even as Malm was saying, "Now we are all Palestinians," Hamas was killing and maiming Fatah members on the Gaza Strip. This confusion about nationalism has wrought much mischief on the Left: after all, how can we know who our enemies are, when we can't even sort out our friends?

What about Denmark? I wondered hopefully. During the Second World War, Denmark bravely stood up to the Nazi demands for Jewish deportations and managed to save most of its Jewish minority. Its record was far better than that of Norway: "our own" police forces, regardless of whether they were servile instruments or willing executioners, rounded up Jews and deported them en masse. Officially Denmark still seems far more sober than Norway.

But the Left terrorism of the Blekingegade group (which was directly related to the Popular Front for the Liberation of Palestine) and the staunch "anti-imperialism" advocated by Maoist and Stalinist parties (and many such sects still exist in Denmark) have created a strong undercurrent that blends with the milieu of the Danish autonomists, the BZ'ers.

And the autonomous scene in Copenhagen shares with Blitz an unwillingness to confront anti-Semitism as a problem – something I witnessed when I lived there seven years ago and participated in extraparliamentary movements on Nørrebro.[16]

In fact, support for the Palestinian cause is dismayingly strong in Denmark among large sectors of the population, and many have taken a stand in favor of the "resistance" in Gaza. This weekend's protests were headed by leading Social Democrats and humanitarians, yet they encountered the same problems – sentiments that run deeper than mere opposition to Israeli policy.

Two recent events are particularly troubling. On New Year's Eve in Odense, two Israeli citizens were shot down in a shopping mall, but luckily they survived. The

---

16. At one point, in one of the groups I was active in, as I saw several problematic reactions by leftists to the Second Intifada, I tried to highlight the issue, forwarding to our discussion group some useful information written by Eric Kraebbers and Jan Tas of the remarkable Dutch antiracist group De Fabel van de Illegal (http://www.gebladerte. nl/30037v01.htm). But I immediately met fierce opposition – members expressly held "all Jews accountable" for everything Sharon and the Israeli government did. After a short but harsh argument, the group agreed to postpone (read: to silence) a discussion of anti-Semitism. The discussion never happened; apparently the issue was too "divisive."

perpetrator was a Palestinian – furious at the invasion of Gaza – according to alleged friends who gave an interview duly masked behind the Palestinian flag.[17] That night these friends threw a party to celebrate the deed. (Does anyone remember the scenes from Gaza on 11 September 2001?)

The second act should concern us even more. Beginning with headmaster Olav Nielsen of Humlehave School in Odense, a number of Danish school administrators have "confirmed that they recommend that Jewish children should not enroll at their schools." Apparently, Jewish pupils have become too grave a security risk.

Still surfing the Net, I found an appalling picture, also from Odense: in a pro-Palestinian demonstration on January 2, a father had dressed up his child as a suicide bomber.[18] In the picture the father wears the colors of Hamas. Although familiar from propaganda videos from the Middle East, such images are – and indeed should be – shocking to Scandinavians.

In an even more disquieting trend in Denmark, a sizable and vocal proponent of fundamentalist Islam has emerged. The party Hizb ut-Tahrir – "whose ideology is Islam" – has been controversial part of Danish political life for some years now. This international organization openly

---

17. The interview in Danish is here: http://www.youtube.com/watch?v=zH4CE338SSA.

18. See http://www.fyens.dk/article/1158134:Fokus—Det-palaestinensiske-selvmaal.

condemns democracy, equality, secularism, and personal freedom as "un-Islamic" and has called for a jihad against Israel and the West. Hizb ut-Tahrir has at numerous occasions denied the Holocaust, and its hatred of Jews is unmistakable.

In the spring of 2002 Hizb ut-Tahrir handed out leaflets in Copenhagen that were threatening to Jews: using a quote from the Koran, the leaflet urged Muslims to "kill them wherever you catch them, and drive them out from whence they drove you out." The leaflet said, "The Jews are a people of slander ... a treacherous people ... they fabricate lies and twist words from their right context." For making such statements, its leader, Fadi Abdullatif, was found guilty of racism by several Danish courts. Usually the party is more prudent in its public statements, but suicide bombings in Israel are consistently described as "legitimate" acts of "martyrdom."

In response to the Gaza offensive, Hizb ut-Tahrir called for "a mobilization of armies to battle" and the recruitment of capable soldiers against the aggression of the "Jewish Entity."[19] The invasion of Gaza, they say, "is an attack on the Muslim community." In fact, for them, the whole of Palestine is "sacred soil."

On 9 January, after Friday prayer, Hizb ut-Tahrir amassed its adherents and organized a massive demonstration in central Copenhagen. Unlike many

---

19. See it, in their own words, here: http://www.hizb-ut-tahrir.dk/new/.

countries in the Middle East and Central Asia, Denmark does not ban this organization, and no police crackdowns meet its public demonstrations. Friday's demonstration was drenched in anti-Semitic slogans and calls for Jihad and for a Muslim Palestine.[20]

On Saturday a different kind of demonstration took place outside the Copenhagen City Hall. Here the fringe elements that tend to show up at liberal anti-Israeli demonstrations revealed more of their political sympathies: to the calls of "Down, down with Israel," one participant raises his arm in a Nazi salute, calling for Hitler, and shouting participants repeatedly proclaim war on Jews.

At one point in the video a jihadist speaker says, "We want to kill all the Jews, all the Jews should be slain: They have no right to exist!"[21]

Again, although I had known that anti-Semitism is simmering in some communities today, I was utterly shocked to find such blatant, overt, and shameless expressions of this age-old hatred.

---

20. See http://www.youtube.com/watch?v=WZ-v_9ONCIw.
21. See, for instance, http://www.youtube.com/watch?v=AeUzAk1nXy4 and http://www.youtube.com/watch?v=fkxF7tOoceA&NR=1. These videos show the Hizb ut-Tahrir flags, and more utterly shocking statements and anti-Semitic slogans than I can list here. Still, I have heard no accounts of autonomists or antifascists confronting Hizb ut-Tahrir or any Islamist street demonstration. On the contrary, as far as I can judge, autonomists are actually present in both of these videos, holding a banner titled "Is this defense?" accompanied by pictures of dead children.

Still, even if we set aside the attacks on and hatred of Jews for a while (unfortunately, many people find this much too easy), why would we accept attacks on basic freedoms that we have gained through centuries of social struggle here in the North of Europe? Even the simple YouTube video clips I've presented here show jihadist Muslims in openly chanting, "Down with Israel. Down with the USA. Down with democracy. Down with Denmark." Why are we not taking them seriously?

In the name of democracy and freedom of expression, we apparently tolerate people openly attacking democracy and freedom. How is that possible? Have we learned nothing from the 1930s? Have we forgotten that the NSDAP gained power in Germany by electoral means, on a program that called for a destruction of that very system? Have we forgotten that the NSDAP promised to purify Germany of the corrupt Weimar Republic and make the country great again? To that end, the Nazis promised the radical youth of the *v*ölkisch movement that they would carry out a political and cultural rebellion *against* democracy and the values of the Enlightenment. Can the rise of Hitler be *excused* – not only explained! – solely by the humiliations that the Versailles Treaty imposed?

This history is mirrored in arguments that legitimate Hamas because it is a "legally elected" government – regardless of the content of its political program. From an antifascist perspective, I cannot see that this argument is valid. How can we ignore the content of jihadist calls for a "final solution" for peace in the Middle

East? The Islamists are quite outspoken about their aims in their documents and speeches – in the Hamas Charter, in numerous Palestinian television broadcasts, and in statements by leading Hamas officials. Why don't we acknowledge the politicized connotations of the *Ummah* in modern Islamist discourse? Why don't we acknowledge the meaning of calls for a "global caliphate"? Islamist political parties don't hide their intentions. What exactly is it that don't we understand about "Sharia," "jihad," and "fatwas" against the *kuffar*, the unworthy "unbelievers"?

Indeed, it is about time we – leftists – ask ourselves why, in our "anti-imperialist" struggle, we seek the company of the most reactionary elements. Do we really hate the United States, Israel, and Western countries that much? Is this the way to move forward, for freedom and peace for Arabs, Israelis, and everyone else on this planet? How can we possibly justify leftist tolerance of radical Islam's misogyny, patriarchy, homophobia; its religious totalitarianism; its anti-intellectualism, anti-secularism, and anti-socialism; its contempt for individual liberties; and its truly poisonous anti-Semitism? Do we really support all these "resistance movements"? Do we understand the full extent of these "unholy alliances"? Are we really willing to sacrifice that much?

Anyone who wants proof of the sincerity of the fatwas might well ask Ayaan Hirsi Ali or maybe Salman Rushdie. After all, we cannot ask Theo van Gogh or Hitoshi

Igarashi. And there are reasons why Ibn Warraq publishes his books under a pseudonym.

Even the "harmless" conflict over a few caricatures in a Danish newspaper claimed some 136 lives. Have we already forgotten that, in response to this "godless act," a leading member of Hamas, Mahmoud al-Zahar, issued death threats? The scenes from Gaza during the Caricature Conflict leave us no reason to think these threats were empty.

Hassan Nasrallah, the leader of Hezbollah, curiously proclaimed that the whole conflict over the caricatures could have been avoided if people loyal to the ayatollah had succeeded in carrying out the fatwa against Rushdie, and thereby frightened people in the West from committing such "blasphemous acts." These calls for Sharia and jihad are the expressed politics of Hezbollah and Hamas, and there is no reason whatsoever not to take their words seriously. And their politics in southern Lebanon and Gaza tell us that we certainly should.

Actually, Norwegians do not have to go to Iran or any other foreign country to see the seriousness of the fatwas. Back in 1993 William Nygaard was shot down outside his house and left for dead, barely surviving after months in hospital. He was the Norwegian publisher of the translated *Satanic Verses*. Nobody was ever caught for committing this heinous act, and police and authorities were most careful not to highlight any evidence that could offend or alienate the Muslim minority. It took them *five years* to publicly *suggest* that the attacks *may* have had something to do with the Iranian fatwa![22]

Such vacillation has been a constant in Norwegian politics ever since, perhaps most embarrassingly in Jonas Gahr Støre's remarkably weak responses to the Caricature Conflict. A variety of militant Palestinian groups were demanding an immediate apology from the Norwegian minister of foreign affairs, or else they would attack Norwegian citizens. As death threats poured in, aid personnel were quickly evacuated from Gaza. Støre might have boldly defied intolerance and unequivocally defended freedom of speech and expression as a founding pillar of the modern, open society; instead he mumbled something about religious feelings being hurt and the need for dialogue.

One placard in a demonstration against the caricatures in Oslo stated, "Your freedom of expression ends the moment you step on my feet."[23] The absurdity of this is simply stunning: freedom of expression begins *exactly that*

---

22. Anyone who believes in the myth of a world Zionist conspiracy is encouraged to compare this case to Norwegian police efficiency in the murder of Ahmed Bouchikhi in the Lillehammer affair of 1973.

23. On 6 February 2006 a rally was arranged in Oslo: see http://www. dagbladet.no/nyheter/2006/02/11/457536.html?i=9. The whole series of photos in *Dagbladet* is quite interesting: Placards with "Islam is the Truth" and "When Truth Comes, Lies Disappear" went together with condemnations of Norwegian Media for "spreading lies." Some 1500 marched in this demonstration, where women were duly relegated to a separate section at the end of the rally.

*moment* you might happen to step on others' feet. Such is the level of contemporary doublespeak. As the originator of this last term, George Orwell, so cleverly put it, "If liberty means anything at all, it means the right to tell people what they do not want to hear."

Orwell, whose books taught us so much about totalitarianism, did not stand idly by as reaction triumphed in Europe. In 1936 he volunteered to fight in the Spanish Civil War, to defend the Republican government against the religious fascism of Franco's Falange and the Carlist Requetés. By joining this struggle, he hoped to defend the ideals of democracy and a libertarian form of socialism.

The failure of his generation to stem fascism in Spain, Italy, and Germany led to the greatest disaster of that century. We must learn from their mistakes.

Norway today is not faced with an impending "Muslim takeover" of any kind, despite what right wing populists may want us to believe. Norway is not subject to covert "islamization" and Europe is not about to become "Eurabia." Still, the dangers of a new religious intolerance – even as fascism – is not exaggerated. Islamists themselves certainly perceive the links between, say, opposition to caricatures of the prophet and a jihad against Jews and the West.

During the Caricature Conflict, angry protesters marched toward the Danish Embassy in London with placards like "Behead the one who insults the prophet" and "Butcher those who mock Islam," together with the simple "Freedom go to hell." Here in London – only seven months after the July 7 bombings – another placard shamelessly read, "Europe, you will pay: your 9/11 is on its way." One burqa-clad protester warned, "Get ready for the *real* Holocaust!"

Hamas, Hezbollah, and other Islamist organizations have repeatedly and unmistakably voiced similar calls. For anyone with eyes to see, the hateful messages are impossible to ignore.

Such calls, I must emphasize, are not the message of Islam. But they are the message of *Islamism*, of so-called political Islam, whose organizations and parties claim Islam as their *political ideology*.

Moreover, militant jihadist groups and parties like Hamas pose a direct and serious threat not only to Jews but to ordinary Palestinian Arabs as well. As self-conscious representatives of the counter-Enlightenment, Islamist political parties constitute a grave threat to freedom-loving queers, women, workers, dissidents, and students in Lebanon, Palestine, and elsewhere. I fail to understand how this fact is lost to the Scandinavian Left, particularly to those who claim to be "anti-imperialists."

Unless antifascists counter these political tendencies forcefully, they will grow, and they will continue to poison all attempts to have any real dialogue or peace and, in the last instance, freedom.

Efforts to undermine the basic rights and freedoms that have been fought for, and won, at such great cost over the centuries demand a renewal of the struggle. This struggle is certainly not about repressing the personal beliefs of individuals. On the contrary, it is a struggle to ensure that individuals continue to have personal beliefs, without fear of either persecution or physical attack.

Reflections:

# 28 Days Later

A few hectic days in January revealed that lingering anti-Semitic prejudices are strong even here in Norway. We must recognize what happened and truly understand the events.

We cannot allow this social disease (and there is no other way of describing anti-Semitism) to spread, for unless we are thoroughly vaccinated and vigilant against it, it will undergo mutations and find new hosts.

To many journalists, political commentators, sociologists, and politicians, the outbursts of aggression may seem random and "without directionality," but they follow the distinct pattern of classic and modern expressions of anti-Jewish hatred. Still, very few commentators have displayed any understanding of the significance of these riots. Indeed, what shook me most was that many left radicals and prominent intellectuals subsequently trivialized them in the media.

That weekend exposed the implications of contemporary hatred of Israel. The Israeli bombing and ground invasion of Gaza was used as a pretext for unleashing violent attacks on Jews and alleged Jewish interests. Of course, no pogroms occurred, and no Jews were killed during the riots, but the incident was in no sense minor; the riots were the most violent Oslo had seen in three decades.

This virus is contagious, and the rage it causes has time and time again proven to be uncontrollable.

Ayaan Hirsi Ali once said, "Tolerance of intolerance is cowardice." I fail to understand how any humanist, left-libertarian, or antifascist could disagree. We cannot allow this hatred to linger in our culture. Whatever form it may take, anti-Semitism must be continually denounced by those who value Enlightenment and humanism.

These riots were the wake-up call.

In our struggle, we cannot opportunistically oppose reaction, as Pastor Niemöller did in the 1930s. Quite often, the enemies of our enemies are not our friends. No, leftists and radical humanists act from principle.

When I challenge parliamentarism, I am fighting for *more* democracy – not less. I genuinely think democracy can be expanded so that all citizens can take direct part in shaping the destiny of society, through further "opening up" our political system, and establishing a system of empowered popular assemblies. I want all our public officials to become more neutral, more transparent, and under stricter civil control. When I oppose the nation-state, it is not from support for a global state; least of all one governed by religious precept, like a world caliphate or the papacy. When I oppose borders between people, it is not because I want reactionaries to take over relatively free societies. When laws against blasphemy are finally removed, they should not be replaced by new restrictions on criticism of religion: when I oppose the Norwegian church and Christian prejudice, it is not because I want to replace it with new kinds of religious intolerance. Rather I want to elevate secularism and generous humanist values: the great promises of the Enlightenment and the democratic tradition must be fulfilled.

Today political and religious forces are working to undermine and fight humanist universalism, democracy, and secularization. In responding to these challenges, we cannot afford to be either reckless, naïve, or cynical. We must remain humanists; yet stand firm.

An open, pluralist society can only be actualized on a secular, common ground, based on freedoms of expression, belief, assembly, and organization. These hard-won freedoms have to be defended. Indeed, they should be expanded, not limited. When reactionaries seek to limit them, our only response can be: *Molon labe* – Just try to take them from us!

We must advance a policy of zero tolerance toward sheer political and religious reaction, and accept no politics of racism, homophobia, or anti-Semitism, no hate crimes. This should not be a Platonic commitment: when mobs roam our streets crying "Death to the Jews," they must be confronted by antifascists, by all means necessary. For the love of Arabs, Israelis, Norwegians, indeed all human beings, we cannot allow fascists, neo-Nazis, or Islamists to gain a foothold in our societies. Like earlier generations of antifascists, we must resist and say: *No Pasaran!* They shall not pass!

We must resolutely oppose the influence of religion in social and political affairs and help society progress toward full secularization. In a secular and open society, people of all denominations can live together. Christianity's historical record is no better than that of Islam – we have to be eminently clear that we do not support a new Inquisition or *La Cruzada* any more than we support calls for Sharia and Jihad. Having curbed the reactionary political influence of religion here in Norway and most other European countries, we must not succumb to the same old garbage draped in new clothing. Today, whenever reactionaries seek to introduce fatwas and Sharia, we must be ready to proclaim loud and without hesitation: *Over our dead bodies!*

Most important, we must fight revisions of the Holocaust. Today Holocaust *denials* are rampant, as they have been in European Nazi circles for decades, but Holocaust *trivialization* and *inverting* are equally dangerous. Whether its source is a neo-Nazi like Horst Mahler, a right-wing historian like David Irving, or a radical Muslim convert like Roger Garaudy; a Muslim politician like the Malaysia's Mahathir bin Mohamad or a socialist one, like Spain's Jose Luis Rodriguez Zapatero; a Catholic bishop like Richard Williamson, or an influential Sunni scholar like Yusuf al-Quaradawi – *it is not acceptable.*

Nor can we underestimate the extent to which traditional and modern anti-Semitism blend together in, say, the writings of a Jostein Gaarder, the movies of a Mel Gibson, or the cartoons of a Carlos Latuff: despite their apparent reputability, celebrity, or radical posturing, all feed into such trivialization and inverting and help set the stage for an all-too-familiar hate politics. When Jews or Israelis are *demonized* and *dehumanized*, we must both expose and oppose it. After all, precisely such demonization and dehumanization cause Quaradawi and other Islamists to call for a new Holocaust.

Whenever anyone calls for attacks on Jews, for the destruction of Israel, or for a new Holocaust, it is our responsibility to raise the antifascist cry of 1945 louder than ever before: *Never again!*

If we fail, our children will indeed avert their faces from us.

# *Looking forward:*
# *Anti-Semitism, Israel and the Left*

Until the end of the Second World War, anti-Semitism was primarily a reactionary phenomenon, espoused by the political and religious Right. This has changed. Now anti-Semitic prejudices are just as common on the Left and are often excused by moderates as well as radicals. Usually today's anti-Semites point to Israeli policy as their main argument, but too often they vilify the Jewish state and Zionism far beyond legitimate criticism.

Obviously, to be *anti-Israel* means more than to criticize some or many actions of the Israeli army, the Mossad, and the Knesset. Too often people judge Jews, Israel, and Israeli citizens according to extremely different criteria than when they are judging *any* other "nation." Frankly I find this double standard puzzling.

Inexplicably, for whatever the state of Israel chooses to do, whether in war or in peace, Jews are always held accountable. No other state or population faces the same charges of complicity and culpability. Absurdly, blame is placed not only on every Jewish citizen of Israel but on every single Jew on this planet! Unfortunately, this is not just a fringe phenomenon but is highly symptomatic of "radical" condemnations of Israel and justifications for anti-Zionism.

Poisoned by stereotypes of the "eternal Jew," justifiable critiques of Israeli policy often spill over into outright condemnations of Israel as such. I have huge problems understanding how Zionism can be interpreted as a synonym for racism, imperialism, and fascism; and I strongly object to popular misconceptions that Israel is based on "apartheid" or even practices a "Holocaust." Such malevolent accusations are alarmingly deceptive.

I am not saying that we must refrain from criticizing Israel or its leaders – indeed, criticism of Israeli policies and actions is often warranted. Nor should we presuppose that all criticism of Israel is anti-Zionist or based on anti-Semitic prejudice. As with any country, we should subject Israel's politicians and officials to close scrutiny and critique. Often its political leadership makes mistakes that have terrible consequences. Does the Israeli Defense Force commit war crimes? Yes, sometimes, and the IDF should be held responsible for them. But to work from the premise that Israel itself is illegitimate, and that the very existence of its powerful army is a war crime, passes from normal criticism to the realm of prejudice.

Similarly, we may legitimately scrutinize and criticize Palestinian governance and oppositional movements – something the Left today too often fails to do. In my view, it is not the responsibility of leftists to support either Zionism or Palestinian nationalism; nationalism *is*, as Oscar Wilde put it, "the virtue of the vicious." But what makes no sense is to seek to eradicate *only one form* of nationalism, namely the Israeli. Those who seek alternatives that are cosmopolitan and internationalist – indeed antinationalist – have no alternative but to expose and oppose both Zionism and anti-Zionism, as well as all oppression and discrimination along religious, cultural, and ethnic lines. But to presume that primarily Jewish nationalism and Israel must disappear to achieve a free society is dangerously wrong.

I deplore the historical conditions that have brought about today's bloody deadlock in the Middle East. But the "anti-imperialist" Left is mistaken in its belief that the solution lies in a further polarization and escalation of the conflict: it is far too enmeshed in national and religious delusions.

In this context any step taken to advance democracy, civil liberties, social equality, and secularism is progressive, because it makes possible finding a necessary common ground. Left-libertarians should support political solutions and peace initiatives that seek to bring stability and security to the region – for all Israelis and Palestinians – which in turn can ultimately be transcended by more progressive forms of social organization. What counts is that Israelis, Palestinians, and their neighbors end up having the leeway to later reorganize society. Today they don't.

How should left-libertarians relate to questions of Israel and anti-Semitism? As a point of departure, here are some basic principles.

First: Anti-Semitism is a despicable and sinister cultural prejudice, with a long and extraordinarily brutal pedigree. It has historically taken a variety of religious, racist, and political forms. It did not emerge with the establishment of Israel or the emergence of Zionism, and linking it to specific Israeli policies or even the existence of Israel helps us neither to understand nor to overcome it. Equally ancient, and equally wrong, is the tendency to put the blame for anti-Semitism on Jews themselves. Neither Israel, Zionism, Judaism, nor Jews are the causes of anti-Semitism or anti-Judaism.

Second: *Regardless of the actions of one, some, many, or even all Jews*, the Left, particularly libertarian socialists, must expose and counter anti-Semitism and Judeophobia. Our humanism and our opposition to hierarchy demand that we soberly reject *all forms of racism, nationalism, and ethnic prejudice*, as well as exploitation or oppression. No biological or cultural essentialism can account for the actions of a given social group or "people." Anti-Semitism is not to be justified or rationalized: it is to be fought.

Third: Israel is not immune to criticism, and much legitimate criticism is in no sense anti-Semitic. Yet strong traditions of anti-Jewish hatred should make us cautious about falling into the more sinister patterns of "criticism." We should demand that Israel be judged by to the same criteria as other nation-states. Whatever our standards are, we should apply them equally to all countries, in the Middle East and in the rest of the world.

Fourth: When a given nation-state commits reprehensible actions, that state's particular citizens or subjects are not to be blamed. During the Second World War it was *Nazism* and *fascism* that we fought, not *the Germans.* Some Germans fought fascism too; and right-wing, nationalistic, and outright fascist movements emerged in many countries before, during, and even after the war. Anti-*German* attitudes were as despicable in 1945 as they are today. What must be criticized and fought is right-wing policies and ideologies, racism, fascism, and totalitarianism, not particular "nations" or "peoples." Not only is this the correct humanist position; it is the only way to prevent fascism from re-emerging, in new forms and from new places. We must not jeopardize our very capacity to stay alert, to comprehend, and offer resistance.

Fifth: We must seek the fullest understanding of political concepts and use them appropriately. *Fascism* is not a word to be tossed around wantonly. Likewise, *anti-Semitism* must be understood and used carefully. Above all, we should be extremely careful today about making comparisons to the Third Reich, Nazism, and genocide, *particularly* to the Holocaust.

Sixth: Anyone can hold anti-Semitic views, including people on the Left and others seemingly "immune" to such prejudices. Even people who are ethnically or culturally Jewish can express anti-Semitic sentiments or viewpoints. Marx's essay "On the Jewish Question" is but one striking example. It is actually not uncommon for Jews to express anti-Jewish sentiments. Our obligation is to look at *the content of the ideas expressed*, not at the skin color, the nationality, or even necessarily the political label of the messenger.

Seventh: The term *anti-Semitism* specifically refers to a fear and hatred of Jews. Arguments about the definition of "Semitic" peoples and languages are irresponsible and an intellectual *cul-de-sac*. However imprecise etymologically, the word *anti-Semitism* was coined by Wilhelm Marr in the 1870s precisely to present anti-Jewish sentiments in a modern, scientific disguise. At the time, traditional anti-Judaism had fallen into disrepute as a form religious intolerance, and a new word was needed to give it credibility. After the Second World War, the word *anti-Semitism* itself fell into disrepute, and new words again had to be coined to present old ideas to new audiences.

Eighth: Anti-Semitism is in no sense the cultural essence of any "nation" or a defining feature of Gentile culture. It is a set of fallacious and irrational delusions. As such, anti-Semitism *can* be understood, confronted, and hopefully uprooted.

Ninth: Every "nation" contains not only class and hierarchical social stratifications but also *political differences.* Like all other peoples, Israelis are split between a Left and a Right, and like all other governments and ministers, theirs can be judged for their political views. To blame Israelis as such for, say, the often extremely reactionary (and deeply religious) sections of the settlers' movement is as dangerous as, say, blaming Lebanese as such for the religious reactionaries in Hezbollah. We must look at the political and cultural influence of the ultra-Orthodox as well as at the Islamists, the general level of secularization and of rights and liberties, when trying to understand political trends and developments in Israel, Palestine and other countries in the region, just as we would expect in "our own" countries.

Tenth: Support for *national liberation* can only be blind. No national liberation movement demands our unconditional support: the extent to which any such movement is *also* struggling for *social* liberation is what conditions our recognition and possible support. Our responsibility should be to support – practically, politically, and ideologically – social liberation movements. Most often, struggles for national liberation replace struggles for social liberation, and too often the so-called Left watches silently or even applauds. Movements for social liberation are sometimes framed in national terms, or given a national form, but the focus, content, and totality of their expressed program are what counts.

Eleventh: Political resistance to policies of the United States, the European Union, NATO, Germany, Israel, Norway – and even countries like Saudi Arabia, Lebanon, Syria, and Iran – must not lead us to support appalling *anti-social* actions like suicide bombings or arbitrary terror against civilians (of a different "nation" as in Israel, or the same "nation" as in Iraq). Even when allegedly used for progressive ends, terrorism is always a substitute for more radical educational and mobilizing efforts. Much of today's Left (apart from the sectors that are entirely liberal or pacifist) has no criteria whatsoever by which to evaluate struggles for *social* liberation and the means employed in fighting what has been (quite problematically) termed the "Empire," the "New World Order," or the "transnational elite," or their various regional manifestations.

Finally: We must never abandon the prospects for a common human future. There is no "clash of civilizations"; dividing lines run through every culture, community, and nation. Despite tempting parochialisms, we must keep our eyes fixed on the potentiality for human recognition beyond all national boundaries, and on universal emancipation beyond all borders – in a libertarian socialist order based on secular standards and an expansive democracy.

A principled Left, rejuvenated by reaffirming Enlightenment universalism and democracy, holds the key to the future, both in the Middle East and elsewhere.

# *Suggested Readings*

Knowledge and education are the best weapons against anti-Semitism. The following works and movies may give a better basis for understanding this phenomenon.

For those who read Norwegian, a good place to start is *Jødehat: Antisemittismens historie fra antikken til i dag*, edited by Trond Berg Eriksen, Håkon Harket, and Einhart Lorenz (Oslo: Damm & Sønn, 2005). This fascinating account is eminently readable and covers the trajectory of anti-Semitism through the ages. Unfortunately, it is not yet translated to English. Scandinavians may complement this work with Henrik Bachner's *Återkomsten: Antisemitism i Sverige efter 1945* (Stockholm: Natur och Kultur, 1999), which gives a better overview of anti-Semitism since the Second World War.

The English-language classic is of course Leon Poliakov's massive work on *The History of Anti-Semitism* (1955–1977: All four volumes were republished in 2003 by The University of Pennsylvania Press).

A brief general introduction to the anti-Semitic worldview and history is *Anti-Semitism: A Very Short Introduction* by Steven Beller (Oxford: Oxford University Press, 2007). Readable is also Walter Laqueur's *The Changing Face of Antisemitism: From Ancient Times to the Present Day* (New York: Oxford University Press, 2006). I have greatly enjoyed everything I read by George L. Mosse but would recommend here his *Toward the Final Solution: A History of European Racism* (Madison: University of Wisconsin Press, 1985). An interesting comparative treatment of anti-Semitism and white supremacy is found in George M. Fredrickson's *Racism: A Short History* (Princeton: Princeton University Press, 2002). Norman Cohn also deserves many readers, as he is insightful as well as readable. His *Warrant for Genocide: The Myth of the Jewish World Conspiracy and the Protocols of the Elders of Zion* (1967; London: Serif Books, 2006), remains a classic exposition of this forgery. (Just before he died in 2005, Will Eisner finished a fine cartoon presentation of it, called *The Plot*.) Recommended is also Marc Levin's documentary on contemporary anti-Semitic conspiracism, called *Protocols of Zion* (HBO, 2005).

About the Holocaust, anyone who cares to look will find an abundance of good, informative books. For a general video overview, I strongly recommend the six-episode documentary, *Auschwitz: The Nazis and the 'Final Solution'* (BBC, 2005; also published as a book), written by Laurence Rees. And, of course, I recommend Claude Lanzmann's masterful documentary, *Shoah* (1985): This 9 1/2-hour oral testimony arguably ranks among the most important films ever made.

A solid humanist critique of contemporary Islam is Ibn Warraq's *Why I Am Not a Muslim* (Amherst, N.Y.: Prometheus Books, 1995). Written in response to the fatwa against Salman Rushdie, it is a layman's introduction, which makes it all the stronger. For an account of Islamism as a political phenomenon, one classic is *Jihad: The Trail of Political Islam*, by Gilles Kepel (Cambridge, Mass.: Belknap Press, 2003; translated by Anthony F. Roberts). Wayne Kopping and Raphael Shore's documentary *Obsession: Radical Islam's War Against the West* (2005) gives a decent overview of the problems of politicized Islam today. It can be viewed together with the three-episode series *The Power of Nightmares: The Rise of the Politics of Fear*, written by Adam Curtis (BBC, 2004), as these two in some ways balance each other. Lawrence Wright's *The Looming Tower: Al-Qaeda's Road to 9/11* (London: Penguin, 2006) brings the jihadists to life and is a most entertaining read.

*Occidentalism: A Short History of Anti-Westernism*, by Ian Buruma and Avishai Margalit (London: Atlantic Books, 2004), gives a brief account of how anti-Western ideas developed in the West as a reaction to modernity. Taking this analysis much further, Matthias Küntzel has documented the links between European National Socialism and Islamist politics in *Jihad and Jew-Hatred: Islamism, Nazism and the Roots of 9/11* (New York: Telos Press, 2008; translated by Colin Meade). This one comes highly recommended. For video lovers, a very good way to spend forty-five minutes is to watch *Blaming the Jews* (Channel 4, 2003). Presented by David Aaronovitch, this documentary gives a sense of anti-Semitism in modern Islamist movements.

Pierre-Andre Taguieff gives an interesting account of recent anti-Semitism in *Rising from the Muck: The New Anti-Semitism in Europe* (Chicago: Ivan R. Dee, 2004; translated by Patrick Camiller). This book was written before the 2005 riots in Parisian *banlieues* and the wars against Hezbollah in 2006 and Hamas in 2009 – events that have increased the problems for Jews in Europe and intensified Judeophobic prejudices. See also Denis MacShane's accessible and informed *Globalizing Hatred: The New Antisemitism* (London: Weidenfield and Nicholson, 2008).

For an antiracist analysis of Left anti-Semitism, I highly recommend Steve Cohen's, *That's Funny, You Don't Look Anti-Semitic* (Leeds: Beyond the Pale Collective, 1984). Kenan Malik renders a fascinating account of British policies of "multiculturalism" since the 1980s in his *From Fatwa to Jihad: The Rushdie Affair and its Legacy* (London: Atlantic Books, 2009); it deserves a wide audience.

Despite the conservative focus of many of its contributors, *Behind the Humanitarian Mask: The Nordic Countries, Israel and the Jews*, edited by Manfred Gerstenfelt (Jerusalem: Jerusalem Center for Public Affairs, 2008), is well worth reading. It documents many of the less savory aspects of the public debate in the Nordic countries; Gerstenfelt singles out Norway's political and intellectual atmosphere as allowing for a variety of anti-Semitic expressions. To some extent, this book documents how the stage was already set for the January 2009 anti-Jewish riots.

Two exciting books that may seem odd in this context are Mark Mazover's *Dark Continent: Europe's Twentieth Century* (London: Penguin Books, 1998), and Eric Hobsbawm's *Nations and Nationalism since 1870: Programme, Myth, Reality* (Cambridge, U.K.: Canto, 1990). Showing how precarious European democracy was during the last century, and how arbitrarily formed the modern nation-states are, both are well worth reading.

These documentaries and books are stimulating and provide a picture of the challenges we are facing. But no bibliography accompanying my account would be complete without any reference to a new, left-libertarian politics. Last but not least I therefore recommend Murray Bookchin's inspiring *From Urbanization to Cities: Toward a New Politics of Citizenship* (London: Cassell, 1995). A more practical exposition is *Libertarian Municipalism: The Politics of Social Ecology*, by Janet Biehl (Montreal: Black Rose Books, 1997). Ultimately, I believe that all forms of racism and xenophobia must be countered by a new, radical humanism that brings political recognition, responsibility, and empowerment to ordinary men and women.

4939236

Made in the USA
Lexington, KY
18 March 2010